Half Way

James Lawton Thompson was born on 11th August 1936, and educated at Dean Close School, Cheltenham. He qualified as a Chartered Accountant in 1959, and did his National Service as a Second Lieutenant in the Third Royal Tank Regiment, 1959-61.

After National Service he studied at Emmanuel College, Cambridge, gaining his M.A. in 1964. In 1966 he was made a Deacon in the Church of England, and served as Curate in East Ham (London). Two years later he became Chaplain at Cuddesdon College, Oxford, and for the years 1971-78 was Rector of Thamesmead and leader of the local Ecumenical Team. In 1978 he became Bishop of Stepney.

Jim Thompson and his wife, Sally, have two teenage children, Ben and Anna. His recreations include painting, a pony and sport.

JIM THOMPSON
Bishop of Stepney

Half Way

Reflections in Midlife

Collins
FOUNT PAPERBACKS

First published by Fount Paperbacks, London in 1986

Copyright © James Thompson 1986

Made and printed in Great Britain by
William Collins Sons & Co. Ltd, Glasgow

Bible quotations in the text are taken from The New
English Bible, Copyright © 1970, Oxford and
Cambridge University Presses.

To Sally, Ben and Anna

Contents

Acknowledgements

Someone may ask how a Bishop of Stepney found the time to write a book. The answer lies in the generosity of many people. Our Archdeacon, Roger Sharpley, and the Area Deans of Islington, Tower Hamlets and Hackney agreed to my having a sabbatical three months to round off my seventh year in Stepney, and then, with others, carried the burdens and "protected" me during that time so that I could write. Most of the writing was done at our home in Mile End, and at Bede House in Kent with the Sisters of the Love of God. In both settings, I was spoilt with love, affection and encouragement.

I thank the Editor of the *Expository Times* for asking me to do the original article, and Sarah Baird-Smith for inviting me to write the book and helping me to believe that I could.

My thanks are especially due to my secretary, Rowena, for typing from my hand-written script, retyping and then revising it yet again. Though sorely pressed, she never complained – well almost never – and completed the work by the due date. The process would not have been possible without her patience and the Archdeacon's word-processor.

When I completed the first draft, I risked submitting it to the scrutiny of my wife Sally, her twin sister Wendy Jennings (rather like travelling between Scylla and Charybdis), my niece Clare, my friend Nadir and my son Ben. I am grateful for the time, energy and skill which they severally gave to the task of constructive criticism. If the book has any virtue, it is because of the expertise of the pruners.

Introduction

When I sit in the Radio 4 "Today" studio, waiting to do "Thought for the Day", I listen to the reports of a whole stream of world events pouring over Messrs Redhead, Timpson and Co. I wonder whether my three minutes and thirty seconds about God and life are going to fit into that stream of life, or be like a brief visit to a stagnant backwater. Sometimes I do feel stranded, but sometimes I sense I'm in midstream, and sometimes it's important to fight against the current. There have been times when I have obviously touched a very sore point, or, without realizing, spoken to a widespread need. I think that happened in the three "Thoughts" I gave on "The in-between times of life". These concerned adolescence, midlife and retirement, and many people experiencing their own crises wrote to me, saying "That's what we want". I was then asked to write an article for the *Expository Times*, and finally to write this book.

My family, supportive as ever, asked what my qualifications for writing such a book were, when there are books by psychologists, psychotherapists, sociologists and doctors.

My first qualification comes from being a bald 49-year-old, who wages a continuous battle against an expanding waistline, who finds himself breathless by the fourth flight of stairs, and feels a direct conflict between the pleasure and comfort of a blow-out at a restaurant and the tale of the bathroom scales. I am now middle-aged, and can begin to look back on what was for me a midlife crisis.

When faced with most of the crises in my life, I have tried to write to myself and pray to God about it, and in my files I found this little meditation which I wrote in 1976. It looks rather pretentious to me now, but it can't quite hide the pain I was feeling:

When love fell in to me and I to it I was overwhelmed,
From God and wife there poured the same sun's showers

Their warmth opened me and I became a man full grown
It was as though the dark side of my earth was brushed in
   light.
But then came thunderous clouds of God and person
   doubt
Which stormed the flickering light and almost blew it out
The clouds were wear and tear, and sleepless nights,
The sameness of the days, the faith dispersed and Church
   worn thin.
The week, week, month, month, year, year of demanding
   others
Which lost my space to be myself, now slowly smothers
The light and life which comes from God and wife.
So my sky raged and flashes of light became a warning of
   the storm to come
And I have had to find a new love of God and wife
Which I must make and share and in deep converse with
   them both,
Find love reborn, redhot and tested in the fire
That youthful hope regained as embers glowing from
   within.

It was a time when the main bases of my life – my faith, our
marriage, my sense of purpose – all seemed to shake at once
and called me to think again about who I was, what I was
doing, and where I was going. My wife and I had been
married for eleven years, I had been ordained for ten, and I
had just had my fortieth birthday, which meant I was on the
way down.

It's taken a long time to work through these issues, and I
don't claim to have solved them, but I am well versed in them
and can look back on a period when they became a crisis for
me. In my twenty years as a priest, I have encountered many
people who themselves have been going through this
turbulent time of life, and my second qualification for
attempting this book is that I have listened to them all and,
from my own vulnerability, tried to counsel them. Priests are
consulted by people who would never dream of going to a

professional counsellor, and there are so many friends and "clients" who have contributed to my own understanding.

Thirdly, there are indeed several disciplines which illuminate our understanding of midlife, such as psychology, sociology and medicine, but I believe that faith, too, has much to offer. Without the dimension of God, the analysis and the answers are stunted. Theology was once thought of as the Queen of Science. It has, for most of my life, been regarded as an archaic and inferior discipline, its insights being regarded with suspicion. A friend of mine provides an example. He has been suffering from mental illness for twenty years, and has had every sort of treatment – group therapy, shock treatment, analysis and, mainly, medication. In those twenty years, he came to depend upon the drugs for anaesthetizing the terror he felt in confronting life. Recently, he has started to come off the drugs. He has started to discover a faith. It is, as yet, just a flicker, but it has been enough to allay the worst of his fear and to help him hope that he will discover within himself the resources he needs to discover meaning and reality in his life. He told me that in all those twenty years no therapist or doctor had ever offered him any idea that he might find a clue in faith, or that spiritual resources were a possible source of strength. In fact, at those times when he had raised the question, this search for faith was regarded by the professionals as a "cop-out", a running away from the tension of the reality which he was thought to be too terrified to face. It was as though they were saying to the hungry man, "You are not hungry, there is no bread". Of course, religion can be a most neurotic response to life, but it is not necessarily so. All those who deny its possibility will have to accept responsibility – if God turns out to be true – that they cut off many a needy human being from the resources of faith, its knowledge, its healing, its strength, its forgiveness, which none of their technology and medicine were able to replace.

Now I detect a growing and welcome humility amongst the "experts". There seems to be a new recognition that we have to take the whole person into account, not just our environment, not just our body, not just our personality, but also our purpose and meaning, the mystery of our motives. Much of the writing about midlife has restricted the faith dimension to critical references in passing. I shall argue that religious insights are essential to the passage through midlife, facing, as they do, questions of destiny, identity and meaning. I make no apology for thinking that theology has a significant part to play. I wish I possessed the knowledge to show how other faiths besides Christianity also have great insights to offer, but that is outside my scope.

My purpose, then, is to examine Midlife and see how the Christian faith can help us tackle it.

1

Midlife – A Time of Crisis?

While I've been writing this book, I've had many conversations about midlife. People in the danger area usually ask "Is it me?" The mean ones say, "That's just what my mother needs", or worse, "That describes my husband exactly". Midlife is not easy to define, but I accept as approximate boundaries what Gail Sheehy called the "Deadline Decade". She wrote:

> Somewhere between 35 and 45, if we let ourselves, most of us have a full-out authenticity crisis.
>
> *Passages – Predictable Crises of Adult Life*, p.350

However, we are all individuals, and our situations and personalities can accelerate or delay any such crisis. Some people may be plunged into it earlier by the loss of a loved one or some other tragedy, whereas others may go on experiencing it till they are fifty, because of a late baby or redundancy or a major change in career. Midlife basically refers to the bridge period into middle age.

But need the midlife be a time of crisis? There are many people who seem to ride serenely through the experience, then find in old age that, having avoided the issues in middle age, they have to pay in their retirement for unexpressed and unresolved tension. For others, it is a very vulnerable period, and can be a time of disaster which does damage that can never be healed. For some, I hope it is a time of crisis which is recognized, accommodated and taken positively into the remaining third of life. When asking myself the question "Is midlife a time of crisis?", I was bound to say that it has been difficult for me – and hundreds of people I have known well – so much so that I would want to call the crisis "normal" and potentially as significant and formative as adolescence.

15

Because most of the people who provide my examples have spoken to me in confidence, it's obviously important that their identity is concealed. Yet I think that it is in the real people and their own struggle that the problem can most clearly be seen. In studying their situation, we may discover the technique for survival, and maybe even turn the crisis into just another stage towards the abundant life which Christ promised us. I would like to describe four examples, taken from life, but heavily disguised.

A woman was educated in East London. She suffered from the low expectations of girls in her school life, and left, feeling that her main purpose was to get married, to look after her husband and bring up her children. This she did. Her relationship with her husband was stormy, but they kept on and on trying to cope with it. But then, between 35 and 45, a set of circumstances happened which caused her to have several years of very great personal crisis. She began to ask questions, which had long been suppressed, about her sexuality. She wondered whether her unsuccessful and unsatisfactory relationship was really due to the fact that she was a lesbian. She saw around her women who had totally rejected the image which had been given to her by her education and class expectation, and she wondered why she should not be allowed to have a fuller life, where she would discover some value beyond her role as a wife and mother. At the same time, her teenage children were at their most difficult. They resented deeply the tension between her and her husband, and seemed to go out of their way to deny even her basic human rights to some life of her own and decent consideration. She wondered whether she wouldn't be better off away from them all, leading her own life, and just for once trying to discover her own identity. She knew that she was fast becoming less attractive, and somehow the approaching menopause seemed to threaten a final bereavement. This was her last chance of an alternative way of life.

So she abandoned home, family and husband, and set up in her own flat, experimenting with relationships as a lesbian and exploring the developments of her own gifts in her working life. This "solution" was unsatisfactory for her, and left her family in shock and hurt. This made her feel that, not only was her new alternative unsatisfactory, but she had also messed up the family in which she had invested her adult life. Her midlife crisis became a crisis for the whole of her family and friends. Yet she knew that there had to be a change, and a change of a fairly radical nature.

*

A man who had done very well in the teaching profession suddenly realized, through a series of incidents, that it was unlikely that he was going to be offered promotion. He had swept through his career to date; he felt a terrific sense of drive and enjoyed the value of what he was doing. Having been in an important position of authority, and nearing the end of his term in that post, he began to think about what he would do next. He saw his friends and colleagues promoted, and began to feel left behind. At first, it was just momentary depression, but then, as the years passed, he began to lose hope. It was difficult for him, because no one spoke to him about his future, which depended on those holding political power in his locality. He began to realize that he was being labelled, and, in the places where decisions were made, he was stereotyped as a person they could not appoint. He sensed that, although he could not see the reasons himself, people obviously felt that there were serious limitations in his ability. He was going to be caught in the trap called the Peter Principle – namely, that people are promoted to the level of their own incompetence. He began to have nagging doubts about his own ability, and to be self-critical and introspective. Because he had reached a certain level of authority, he found it difficult to share his problems with anyone else. He felt that his wife was rather unsympathetic, and she on her side began to resent his depression. It became a vicious circle, because he became more embittered, and in public debates more cynical. People began to picture him as a moaning and negative influence.

One day he realized that he was going to be in his present job for the rest of his life if he could not find a sideways or downwards move – and people were highly suspicious of candidates who applied for such posts. He had twenty-five years to go before retirement, and he did not feel able to face the possibility of staying in the same post. It affected the whole of his life. He began to spend more and more time on his own, and his interest in his job waned. The crisis was complete when the authorities confronted him with what he was fast becoming, by offering him a deputy headship which would write off as worthless his skill and his experience.

*

A woman who had been to a grammar school and been inspired with a vision of the professional woman, won a place at university and devoted her energies to a career as a nurse. She obtained an excellent degree and, in spite of opportunities to have boyfriends, always responded with considerable reserve to their attentions. For ten years, she did a thoroughly satisfactory and worthwhile job, and would have described her life as fulfilling. She was promoted and began to be given very demanding responsibility. In her early thirties she toyed with the idea of marriage, but her life-style never allowed enough space for relationships to develop. One promotion after another meant that she was always stretched. In her mid-thirties she began to be anxious, and to take steps to find a more permanent male friend. However, the demands of her nursing, and her own feelings of fear at growing older, began to show. She tended to dress younger than her age, and made a fool of herself with younger men who were just out for a good time. In her early forties she was ill, and was told that she had to have a hysterectomy because of a cancer. Somehow this symbolized for her the loss of the other self she had not chosen. It was not a choice she could change, and there was a terrifying finality. Her approach to the operation was not just one of fear of the medical implications, but a fear of losing herself and her own unfulfilled womanhood. She began to withdraw from what had filled her life, and she became extremely depressed. Although the operation was successful, and there was no more cancer, her spirit was chronically disabled, and there had to follow a long period of readjustment, accepting her grief, finding a way of facing her future as a spinster, and rediscovering a sense of purpose and direction in her career.

*

A married man had taken the risk of moving from a council house into owning his own home. This move became possible because of a rise in his own salary and his wife finding a job, but the move had cost them more than they had intended, and they were very near the limits of what they could afford. In addition to this, their car was having an old-age crisis, and their teenage children were intelligent and wanted to go into further education. For a while, he was excited and stimulated by the move and the new responsibility, feeling that he was in control and going up in the world. But they had taken on more than they could afford, and he began to work a great deal of overtime. His wife's work, and the long hours he spent at the firm, prevented them from spending time together. They had had a good relationship, based on regular and good communication and enjoyment of each other's company. But he began to worry and found it difficult to talk. It seemed as though whenever they were together, he and his wife only talked about their problems. It affected their sex life, they made love less often, and, if they were truthful, it was unsatisfactory for them both. He found it difficult to cope with the fact that he was not only having to work extra hours to pay off the mortgage, but when he went home it was either a rehearsal of their combined worries, or no one was there at all. He began to feel lonely.

It seemed ridiculous – he had a job, a wife and family, but he felt desperately alone. Then he fell in love. She was much younger than he was, there was a twenty-year age difference. But she made him feel young, and he rediscovered his own younger self. When they met, there was always a sense of affection and sensuality. He began to find all sorts of ways of meeting with her. Somehow she helped him to forget that he was financially hard-pressed, that he was no longer handsome, and they found together a mutual enjoyment which was pure bliss. But it raised for him a whole series of complications. He lied about money, and about where he was, and he began to lead two different lives. He felt he was being offered a second and last chance of happiness. His marriage had only led to a rather stale and tired relationship, drowned in responsibilities, without the fun or the feeling of well-being, a drab sex life, a sense of impending old age and a taste of death. He went on in this divided world, and finally, after two years of deception, he broke down and told first his doctor, then his priest, pouring out all the stress which had nearly killed him.

*

These four examples are not isolated. They represent the hundreds of personal stories I have listened to, and I recognize as I write that I can identify personally with some of the tensions and conflicts, as well as the negative feelings, which they describe. The experience of these cases, taken with my own, makes me believe that there is often a midlife crisis, and leads me to try to understand the causes, in the hope of finding techniques for survival, and maybe even fulfilment.

The first cause of midlife difficulties is the fact that it involves a physical transition. Although youth has its pitfalls, it is often a beautiful time – especially in retrospect – and it is difficult to let go. We can experience longing that we could be young again, and watch with helpless desire and envy as our own body shows signs of wear, and the young look younger and younger every year. For women, the menopause is, perhaps, the most powerful focus of this change, and some experience it almost like a bereavement. The woman who had the hysterectomy experienced a deep sense of loss, not just of the potential to bear a child, but also of her essential self. The menopause can bring not only emotional turmoil, but also sharpen the tell-tale signs of incipient physical decay. Even with the most expensive techniques, these signs can only be momentarily delayed. For the man, there is no such clear physical landmark, and the change is more external but can be equally dispiriting. Perhaps he has been a sportsman – his performance begins to wane, and he has to rely more on cunning and less on physique. He becomes aware of middle-aged spread and loses his hair. Both men and women may try to compensate with smarter clothes and sundry skilful devices, but none of us can put the clock back. We can, of course, put the clock forward by the misuse of our bodies and by failing to prevent disease. Overeating, lack of exercise, smoking, heavy drinking, can all contribute to premature decay, or even, in many cases, to midlife becoming endlife.

It is not only the fact that our body threatens us with crisis, but also at the same time our dependants tend to be going through their own times of transition. Our children will usually have reached, or just passed through, adolescence, and our parents will often be facing their retirement, or be coming to that period of life when the body is becoming a burden and a source of pain and restriction. This can mean that, at the same time as our midlife crisis, we have to face a set of conflicting demands. We need a bit more personal space to cultivate our own relationships, and yet every moment of spare time carries a responsibility to our children or our parents. We need more mutual affection, yet the tension and pace of teenage children makes life seem like an air terminal in a disaster movie. Just when we are feeling sexually tired, and perhaps bored, our children are living it up, and taking it out on us during their pit-stops at home. When we look at our own parents, we see a picture of what we ourselves shall all too soon be going through as our tape speeds up the nearer we get to the end. Alongside our own personal anxiety, there are anxieties about both our children and our parents, a rich soil for guilt to grow in.

So our body and our relationships go through a difficult

phase, just at the time when our role in life is bringing us to a self-evaluation crisis. Midlife seems to be a time when we ask ourselves "What are we worth?", "Where have we got to?" We may regret the choices we've made in the past, and begin to feel especially worthless. Not only are we getting older and feeling it, but we also find it difficult to see what we've really achieved. "I'm only a housewife", "I'm afraid I never went to university", "They say you're over the top at forty", "Don't you think it's time to stop pretending to yourself?" . . . The message conveyed to us over and over again is that we've moved into a different gear, although in our heart of hearts we may still feel as though we are seventeen. I remember what a boost it was to my morale when I was made a Bishop, because everyone started to say how young I was, but I knew that on the squash court I was struggling, and my friends from army days were already finishing that career and looking for jobs in civilian life. So, for many people, midlife seems to be the last chance to choose an alternative life, when regrets about lost opportunities come to a head. We either see the alternatives through a haze of rose-coloured sentiment, or feel despair about the existence to which we have descended. We look desperately for a new start, a new relationship, a new set of values and rejuvenation. The mirror tells us that we are not what we were, and its cold analysis gives substance to the fears which haunt our private thoughts.

Midlife, as its name suggests, is a sort of crossroads between one half of our life and the second – or, for some, between two thirds and the other third. It becomes the bridge between our past and our future in a way which causes many of us to feel stress. How we cope with it will make a considerable difference to the way we experience middle age and growing old. Although it can be a crisis, it can also be an opportunity when we make a new discovery about the purpose and meaning of our lives, and face the positive potential of the remaining stage of our life-span on this earth. How we tackle it can lead us into greater maturity, and perhaps even more serene middle age, or plunge us into personal chaos which is permanently damaging, not only for us as individuals, but also for many of the people around us.

2

" . . . Like a Flower of the Field"

Perhaps it may seem too down-to-earth to begin with our Body. But then, the human being is an earthly creature. I am encouraged by our faith to believe that our body is very significant. The Christian faith teaches that God was in Christ – that in Jesus we see God made human. This faith, built on its Jewish roots, has rejected those who have thought that the body was just a shell for the soul, best soon discarded, and hopelessly tainted with sin and corruption. Not only in the birth of Jesus can we see this:

> The Word became flesh and lived among us.
>
> John 1:14

but also in the Resurrection, there is an assertion of the significance of the Body:

> Touch me and see; no ghost has flesh and bones as you can see that I have.
>
> Luke 24:39

Not only is there the faith that God saw through a Man's eyes what mankind sees, but also that Jesus, shortly before His death, saw His Body as the means of communication through the form of bread and wine:

> This is my body, which is given for you.
>
> 1 Corinthians 11:24

But I begin with the body, not just because the Christian faith directs that I should take it seriously, but because we do take our bodies seriously from the beginning. As babies, we are only interested in sleeping, feeding and being comforted –

working the system! This is a key period of our lives, and we
form infantile habits which die hard. Our bodies are a major
fact of our life from the cradle to the grave, and they merit
attention. We explore them, contemplate them, use them,
abuse them. Although I understand that all protein in the
body is turned over every six months, and when we meet
someone we have not seen for six months there is not one
molecule in his face which was there when we last saw him,
nevertheless we each feel in an unique way "my body is me".
We feel disturbed, and even deranged, when we feel "out of
our body", unless as a result of some higher spiritual or
aesthetic experience. It is also true in my experience that
teachers of religion have been very shy about bodies – almost
as though it would have been better if we didn't have them.
For most of my life, I believed that my body and religion
pulled me in opposite directions, unless, of course, I could
find some nice girl and settle down. At school the idea seemed
to be "play hard, work hard and your body will look after
itself". It's a strange symptom of this split between our
physical and spiritual selves that people often treat priests as
though they somehow managed to leave their bodies behind
at the altar when they were ordained.

I begin with the body because it is the vehicle of our life,
and it's no good knowing how to drive if you don't pay
attention to the car. The body is also one key place where
midlife catches up with us. In youth, we are moving towards
the prime of our physical life, and then, for quite a long
period, we consolidate by being strong and more mature, and
hardly think about growing old, except as a joke. But then we
begin to notice the lines on the face, the baldness, the loss of
our figure, the breathlessness, the creaking joints, the
realization that we can't wear certain clothes any more, the
unintentional and intentional hurts we receive from the
younger generation about our appearance. There is a physical decline, and it can lead to all sorts of unstable behaviour.
It can make us feel panic that "this is my last chance"; "soon
I'll be no longer attractive"; "I'm losing my powers". So we
witness the sad comeback of boxers and athletes; the love

affairs with someone younger than we are; the introspection about the nature of our sexual fulfilment or deprivation; the anxiety which only makes matters worse by comfort-eating or escapist drinking. It is a vulnerable time, when in one sense we are grieving for lost youth and mourning the prime of our physical life.

It's my belief that we are right to attend to our physical development. Our body is an ever-present reality of our life. It has immense influence upon us – as we become only too aware if we experience pain or, through severe illness or accident, lose the use of any major function. It is not only essential in a functional way, in terms of health and fitness and the effect they have on our capacity to share in a full life, but the body and its demands can also dominate our very selves by incessant reminders of its need for basic satisfaction. The person paralysed can be imprisoned by his body; the blind, the deaf, the impotent, the arthritic, are all subject to the potential domination of their body over their very self. Whilst most people do not have these afflictions, all people have to face the fact that physical decay is part of the system in which we are involved, and its cry is heard with increasing force from midlife onwards. The old age and death of our parents faces us with the reality of our own death, whose shadow shakes the security of our own self-understanding.

But the body is not just an ever-present reality with immense power over us, it is also a most significant focus of our self-appraisal. From the moment the little girl parades her new dress, or waits anxiously for her breasts to develop – or the boy combs his hair forty times a day, follows the fashions of his peer group, or hopes his voice will break – we are set on a journey of self-appraisal. It is not only a matter of "how we appear to ourselves", but also "how we appear to others". When interviewing people for jobs, it's important to remember that we may be tempted to appoint the wrong person because he or she is attractive to us. When deciding whether or not to trust someone, it's amazing how often we feel more like trusting the physically attractive person. The advertisers are not foolish when they present to us the image of the dynamic, perfect physical specimens as somehow being the people who are leading the real lives, and by inference suggest that all the rest of us, with sagging waistlines, shapeless suits and imperfect complexions, are missing out on the best of life. They create an image and an appetite which an honest look in the mirror, or the courageous journey to the scales, or the innocent jibe of our children, informs us is no longer ours for the taking. So it is that we begin to reappraise our bodies, and recognize that what pride we have managed to muster in our physique, our appearance and attractiveness, has severely diminished and left us with a low self-image and, as a result, a poor self-evaluation. We may enjoy the advantages of midlife, but for a while none of them really seem to compensate for losing the prime of our physical life.

The Bible has some fairly abrasive words to us about our natural life-cycle, and they are words which are especially important when we begin to experience physical decline. The first assertion, in the Book of Genesis, is that the physical, material world is good:

> God created man in his own image; . . . male and female he created them. God blessed them and said to them, "Be fruitful and increase, fill the earth and subdue it . . ." So it was; and God saw all that he had made and it was very good.
>
> Genesis 1:27,28,31

"God saw all that he had made and it was very good." It was that affirmation of the value and goodness of material life which warded off other ideas that somehow all physical natural life was wicked and that the valuable spark inside us was trapped in a physical prison. So we are encouraged to have a healthy appreciation and respect for our bodies and the natural world around us.

The second story of the creation goes further and shows that man is "of the earth", that he is very much part of nature, and is of the same substance as the earth in which he lives:

> Then the Lord God formed a man from the dust of the ground and breathed into his nostrils the breath of life.
>
> Genesis 2:7

Thus man became a living creature. We are part of nature, and we ignore this fact at our peril. Man has tried to show he is superior to the rest of nature and, because nature is so transient, he has often found it uncomfortable to see himself as subject to its laws. Yet from the first insight that man is made from dust, the mortality of man and his inescapable place in the cycle of nature is confirmed. From the moment of the inbreathing of life till the last breath when we return to the earth, we are earthly, natural creatures. Those of us who lead funerals are often reminded of this fact by the use of Psalm 103:

> For he knows how we were made,
> he knows full well that we are dust.
> Man's days are like the grass;
> he blossoms like the flowers of the field:
> a wind passes over them, and they cease to be,
> and their place knows them no more.
>
> Psalm 103:14–16

This, at first sight, is a solemn reminder of our transience, but I think there can also be a deep comfort in the recognition that we are all part of the natural order. People who live close to the land, and who are much nearer to the natural cycles and rhythms, seem to treat birth and life and death in a much more accepting way. The seasons bring the wonder of new life, the blossom, the fruit, and the quiet comfort of the leaves returning to the earth and received by it. Why should it be so fearful to share the rhythm of the natural creation? What's so terrifying about it? That's the nature of the earth in which human life is possible.

There is a famous passage in the words of the melancholy

preacher – the Book of Ecclesiastes:

> For everything its season, and for every activity under heaven its time:
>> a time to be born and a time to die;
>> a time to plant and a time to uproot;
>> a time to weep and a time to laugh;
>> a time to embrace and a time to refrain from embracing.
>
> Ecclesiastes 3:1,2,4,5

This seems to me to be an important clue for those in midlife – the acceptance of our place in the natural order and our acceptance of the time it is for us. As an ex-teenager, I must remember that I have had that time of life; as a midlife person, I must remember that if I live, I shall become elderly – to everyone their time and their place in nature. Jesus teased the people of all generations when they fought against the boundaries of their natural existence:

> Is there a man among you who by anxious thought can add a foot to his height? If then you cannot do even a very little thing, why are you so anxious about the rest?
>
> Luke 12:25–26

This in no way suggests that we should not care for our body, take all practical steps to prevent flab and stress, to keep as fit as we can, but rather reminds us that we will be happier if we accept the natural characteristics and limitations of the stages through which our bodies pass. There is a beauty to every stage of life, just as the year-cycle of the tree provides us with new buds, full blossom, and bare tree against the winter sky. We are part of the same system, with the added burden and potential of self-consciousness. I am not minimizing the pain and distress of the decaying process in human beings, but rather trying to remind myself that I am a child of the earth and I share its course.

Because the Christian faith has invested so much of its teaching in the Resurrection, it is my belief that we tend to skip over the comfort of God's creation and our being part of it. It is amazing and important to me how healing it is to feel a part of nature. Maybe it is a reaction to city life, where the seasons almost pass us by, but the intense experience of the natural world is like "coming home", a losing of self in the space and interdependent life of nature around me. Not only does it slow me down and help my body to find peace, but also it fills my whole being with what can only be described as a sort of harmony, in which for a while I know how to play my part.

There is comfort in being part of nature and accepting it, but for the person who does not believe in God, there remains the threat of the "nothing" which lies beyond the grave. If there is no resurrection, then "nothing" is what we would encounter – but because it is nothing, because there is no brain activity, we do not encounter it. In itself, it is not a threat – the threat is derived from the loss of all we have come to value. The fear of death, and the ultimate nothing for which we are heading if there is no resurrection, is the menace of the loss of our lives. We may be persuaded of our immortality when we are young, but in midlife there are stronger hints that we are turning towards the end of life and that the pace is quickening.

For the person who believes in God, and especially for the Christian, death is viewed in a different light, because of the faith in the dimension of God. This faith cannot be delivered neatly wrapped like an insurance policy, to remove completely the anxiety caused by the fear of death, but it is a revelation which can put the journey of our body through this life's cycle into perspective. I have found it an enormous encouragement to meet such a faith in those who have nearly reached the end of their own pilgrimage, and who have hope, humour and trust about the world to come.

It is hard with our contemporary materialistic assumptions to imagine "heaven" – God's place – God's dimension. Yet maybe the gate of our minds will be opened by the incredible parable of our technology. The lasers, the microchips, the radio waves, should have shaken us out of the prevailing view that we should only believe what we can touch or see or measure. It is reasonable to assume there might be dimensions of being which we have not yet managed to record on our instruments. It has been one of the strongest ideas of mankind that there is a dimension of God, and the Christian believes that in some way Jesus crossed the boundary and opened the kingdom of heaven. The stone was rolled away and we were allowed a glimpse of Jesus alive in a different way. Yet although He was different, He demonstrated a marvellous continuity with His earthly life and personal experience.

St Paul believed he knew in himself this eternal Christ – that he enjoyed the active love of the Risen Jesus and felt the thrill of His company. He spent much of his life trying to explain and describe what he had experienced and what it meant for us all. He spoke in the most naturalistic terms. He affirmed the earthly life and yet asserted that our true and final destiny, though tasted in this life, was only found when we die:

> . . . flesh and blood can never possess the kingdom of God, and the perishable cannot possess immortality.
>
> 1 Corinthians 15:50

> And when our mortality has been clothed with immortality, then the saying of Scripture will come true: "Death is swallowed up; victory is won!"
>
> 1 Corinthians 15:54

The heavenly life will be a new creation:

> There are heavenly bodies and earthly bodies; . . . what is sown in the earth as a perishable thing is raised imperishable. Sown in humiliation, it is raised in glory; sown in weakness, it is raised in power; sown as an animal body, it is raised as a spiritual body.
>
> 1 Corinthians 15:40,42–44

This is a great vision of the raising to new life with God of the human being who has lived out his natural life on earth. We are pointed both to the fact of earthly life and inevitable death, and, at the same time, are promised a heavenly existence. Just as midlife warns us of our mortality, so faith offers the hope and encouragement that mortality is a preparation for immortality. As we sit by our parent's death bed, or think seriously about our own death and the loss of those we love, there is great comfort to be found in this faith. The fact that it is comforting does not make it untrue.

The acceptance of the time-scale of our body, and the hope of eternal life, are clues we are given as we observe our physical body begin its downward journey. If we attend to their meaning, we may well discover the inner beauty which fills the ugly with grace, the decaying with life, and the fearful with hope. This can challenge our low self-appraisal. It questions our values and judgements and alters our view of the journey itself. We all have to pass through the same cycle – we could damage our integrity and reputation resisting it, or we could begin to suggest that there is a self within us which accepts the time and hallows it, and demonstrates what it is like to be "at home" in each stage of life, bringing considerable riches to those around us and, by our acceptance of ourselves, learning how to accept others. The youthfulness of others can become something which does not have to be envied by those in midlife, but can be enjoyed. The experience can be a preparation for the recognition and acceptance that are so essential to peace of mind in old age. There is an inevitable "giving-up" of more youthful activity, but we are often so reluctant to let go. The body has great power over us, but we must search for the inwardness which enables us to "drive it" within its bounds and natural capabilities. We must take into ourselves, into our spirit and attitudes, the fact of the transience of bodily experience, and live realistically according to its rhythm. Others will then see us as a resource, a source of strength, because we have overcome and accepted our time.

3

The In-between Age

Even if, in midlife, we sort ourselves out and negotiate a way through our own identity crisis, it is often a time of life when our children and parents are experiencing their own problems. The children may well be going through adolescence, and our parents may be facing the upheaval of retirement or just the trials of the ageing process. It is often the case that these pressures combine to aggravate the problems of those caught in the middle, who can feel frustration because they desperately need some space. What space and energy they have is then consumed by the others' needs.

The children's passage through adolescence into adult life can present a special challenge, and it can open up the sores of the midlife wounds. Just when we are beginning to lose our youthfulness and are having to fight a bit harder to maintain some sense of physical well-being, our young are coming towards their peak. They have difficulties about transitional uncertainty, but their physical prime lies ahead of them with all its promise. It is not unusual for there to be an uncomfortable rivalry when the midlife parent sees the children growing up so much freer and with so many more opportunities. The next generation always appears to have it so much better, and "they are not a bit grateful". The younger generation now is facing unemployment and a seriously curtailed future, and that poses a different problem. But in physical terms, just as the midlife person is in descent, the teenager is ascending. The son spends a lot of time making his hair interesting; the midlife dad spends money trying to achieve a minimal cover-up. The daughter may spend hours making herself beautiful; her mother can't do up the button on last year's jeans, and can't remember when she last had her hair done.

It is not only youthful physiques which can seem a bit of a

threat, but the necessary change in the authority pattern can also produce tension. As the youngsters grow more determined to have some independence it will be battle stations. If there were discipline problems before, they can now become a source of crisis.

It is an art to be able to change from the parent who is providing the secure and stable framework for a pre-adolescent child, into the parent who wants to let the post-adolescent young come to full maturity and learn the costly way of standing on their own feet. We have spent the first decade-plus of their lives giving them experience, education and protection – making many of the decisions which affect them, setting boundaries and guidelines for what they may or may not do. Then we have to change gear and enter a new phase, when they will want increasingly to make their own decisions, pushing back the boundaries and guidelines according to their own understanding. The difficulty is caused in part by the fact that they claim understanding and knowledge which we believe they do not yet possess. They will be clear about things which we, in midlife, are just learning are far from clear. Even the most loving families can look at each other across the generation chasm in amazement that their parents or their children could think such things, let alone say and act upon them.

In tackling the problem of values and authority, it is important for the parents to understand their own motives and ask themselves, "What's making me so angry?" The parents in midlife may well be asking themselves whether they dealt with their own adolescence in the right way. There may be a lot of "I wish I hadn't . . . " or "I wish I had . . . " in their reassessment of their own life story. Perhaps they married very young, perhaps they were over-protected and missed out on teenage excitements, perhaps they went through a disastrous period of relationship with their own parents. This teenager in themselves will still be alive and well in their midlife personality. It will probably create a desire "to make sure our children don't go through what we went through and don't make the same mistakes", and will sometimes cause a little resentment that they are negotiating the teenage years with so much more skill and freedom than their parents did.

Then there's the "irresponsibility" of the young – they come in late at night and they threaten our relationship with our neighbours, or bruise our eardrums with their music, and they don't seem to realize that someone has to pay for the heating or the 'phone. Yet here we are – the abused parents, worrying about paying for their clothes, trying to remember what big bills will arrive when, and worrying about financial survival. We also feel responsible for the home, we want it to be a more comfortable and orderly place as we notice and value more what our home is like – and they don't seem to care, leaving trails of unsavoury clothes on the stairs, or leaving their room looking as if it had been burgled. Again, this can be a sore point for midlife parents, because they may be feeling weighed down by responsibilities at work and at home, and sense that they alone are trying to hold the home together and keep it decent.

So the midlife parents will often be feeding into the arguments a substantial amount of their own anxiety about themselves, and their children will reflect back to them the reverse side of their own fragile predicament. This can make it difficult for insight and experience to be passed on.

In a community which has a stable history or where values go for long periods without change, the passing on of tradition, faith and morality is taken for granted. Specific religious groups and societies emphasize the wisdom of elders and the necessity of respect. In Judaism, for example, there is the commandment:

> Honour your father and mother, that you may live long in the land which the Lord your God is giving you.
>
> Exodus 20:12

but also, within the whole working of the home and the synagogue, the element of handing over the tradition is written into the sacred practice. The Passover meal enshrines the part of the children, and this is in some sense a symbol of continuity, tradition and obedience:

> When your son asks you in time to come "What is the meaning of the laws which the Lord our God gave you?" you shall say to him "We were Pharaoh's slaves in Egypt" . . .

Deuteronomy 6:20–21

The identity of the Jewish people in their dispersion has been maintained in this way. But when this religious cohesion encounters the contemporary society, the values and the authority are immediately under pressure. The turmoil comes in part from the pace of change in moral attitudes, partly in the multitude of moral answers to the questions asked, and partly in a fundamental change in the nature of authority itself. For example, parents who came from the West Indies, with a discipline, sometimes enforced by corporal punishment, and a strong Christian faith, encountered crises when their children grew up in the United Kingdom. They were freer to make their own decisions and had a totally different attitude to authority in families and schools, and they found religion in decline. The rebellion has been hard to cope with.

It is not just the experience of immigrant communities, because there are very few families which have not been affected by the changes. People seem to react in two main ways: there are those who will say that the rebellion is a result of abandoning proper respect for parents and teachers, of removing the sanctions and disciplines which kept the child/teenager, for their own good, on more secure behavioural tramlines. On the other hand, there are parents and teachers who recognize that we all have to live with considerable uncertainty in our age. They would claim that the proper approach is to respect the teenager's individual point of view and decision-making, so that the relationship becomes less one of authority and more one of discussion and negotiation. "We'll talk it over and come to a decision together."

Christians and people of other faiths are sometimes called upon to produce certainties, but if we look deeply into most issues there is little certainty about, and people holding the same faith often seriously disagree over what is right and wrong. If we list such issues as trial marriage, homosexuality, our national investment in nuclear weapons, the issues of unemployment and life-styles, we can see immediately that we are in a time of rapid and bewildering change. If we add to this the critique that the young people have expressed against the materialism of the generations since the war, the result is often a complete rejection of values and a dropping out from the life-style and values of the parents and the parents' parents. I have frequently been struck, as I listen first to parents complaining about their teenage children and then to the other side, how often the spiritual search of the young has been the more profound. Perhaps, in the years after the war, people felt that freedom comprised not having a war together with the re-establishment of material and domestic comfort and security. As generations have passed, this has become less satisfactory, leading either to a youthful rejection of materialism and experimentation in a spiritual adventure, or to the unrealistic demand that material expectations should be met here and now. In either case, the expectation of the young adults may be in conflict with the expectation of their parents, and bring stress. So often in this struggle, parents are as inconsistent as their children. A parent will often treat a child like an equal and have a happy, relaxed, "no distance" relationship – but then, when it comes to a particular issue, try to reintroduce the heavy hand. Or, alternatively, they may try to exert the heavy hand, but the child of spirit finds that his peer group will have none of it, and this in turn leads to the rejection of the parental authority. It is my belief that the education system has been made the scapegoat here for what is at root a basic failure in the family.

I do not believe that either the absence of restraint or the use of the big stick are appropriate models for us to follow.

There seems to be something lacking in society where there is no respect for the parents' experience and authority, yet it would be sad to retreat from the basic respect for the teenager's own growing independence. The skill seems to be in knowing how much freedom of decision to allow at each stage. The repressive parent in today's society will often push children into open rebellion, yet the parent who takes no responsibility but lets the children live totally their own way and buys them off, will not provide the necessary security and boundaries. St Paul set out a rather useful mutual relationship:

> Children, obey your parents, for it is right that you should. "Honour your father and mother" is the first commandment . . . You fathers, again, must not goad your children to resentment, but give them the instruction and the correction, which belong to a Christian up-bringing.
>
> Ephesians 6:1–4

So a relationship of trust has to be built up in which the boundaries of the child's freedom are worked out, so that there can be real, stable parental response. Obviously profound disagreement between parents will undermine any authority, as will the obvious hypocrisy of the contrast between their own life-style and what they expect of their children. It is not much use forbidding children to smoke if the parent smokes, to respect the truth if the marriage is based on deceit, or to demand responsible caring behaviour if there is none in evidence. This need is most clear in the handing on of religion. It sometimes seems to me that whole generations have lost the reality of God because their parents believed that faith was good for their children, but not for themselves.

I was once asked to see a teenage boy, expelled from school because of homosexual practice. His father came to me first and ranted at me about the disgusting behaviour of his son. I felt he expected me as a priest to give the boy a hell-fire sermon. As I listened to him, I realized that he was a womanizer, who publicly shamed his wife, who used her as a skivvy and frequently hit her. It was difficult to avoid the conclusion that the boy had been terrified of him from his infancy. Parents often cannot see the totally double standards they apply – one way of life for the children, and another for themselves.

So the priorities for the parent would seem to be a recognition that children need consistency, recognizable boundaries, space and time for relaxation together and an authentic life-style. It is no use either handing over false certainties, or opting out of having any real values and principles at all. It may be that we are offering our children no solid basis for their life, because ours is so directionless and fickle. Part of the process too will be the proper and fair treatment of other members of the family and the family home. The husband who constantly undermines his wife before his children will not help them to respect her themselves. The mother who repeatedly makes her children's decisions for them should not expect them to grow up being responsible and independent.

Children are under so much pressure from their peer groups and the propaganda of the media. Their morals are exposed to influences other than those of their parents, who rapidly become the force of reaction, the nagging killjoys out to spoil everything. In the face of this, it is important for the parents to understand their own predicament and contain the anxiety, because neither dictating nor abdicating will provide the youngsters with the rock they require.

As the children move towards maturity, so their independence and responsibility must develop. The transition will happen most easily where the children have been encouraged all along to stand on their own feet little by little, in ways appropriate to their age and personal development. It is almost impossible for the desire for independence in the young adult to synchronize with the parents' willingness to let go. In the happiest families there will be arguments as each tests out the other. But whatever the pace adopted, the child has to become an adult, and that will mean making decisions and taking steps which are appropriate to their own generation, and which clash with their parents' views. Unless the decision is to do something criminal, indulge in self-destructive addiction or do some manifest wrong, then the integrity of the young adult has to be respected. The house itself can become a focus of this clash. "I respect your right to do it, but not in my house." The use of the home is a very strong sanction. To use that sanction is a desperate throw for any parent because, faced with the choice, too many young people choose to walk out.

Another sanction is money. The teenager's need of money can tempt the parent with money to use bribery and blackmail as a means of control. The parent who is poor will often experience a sense of failure and inadequacy. As in the whole of our lives, the way we deal with money and assess its value speaks volumes about us. The parent often wants to help the children bypass the need for experience, and so expects them to act as if they had had the extra twenty years of learning and paying the bills. The teenager can reflect the family's approach to money sometimes by adopting it wholesale, or sometimes by going to the opposite extreme as a way of expressing rebellion. We live in a sickeningly divided world of poverty and affluence. That is an issue that no family should avoid, and it is imperative that all the adult and nearly-adult members should have developed an understanding of what that means in practical terms for them. If possible, we should help teenagers begin to have money of their own so that they can learn how to use it and put it in perspective. It is perfectly fair to explain why some things are possible and others not, and to help teenagers face economic reality, whilst not dictating the way they spend their own money. It is not only the parents who can use money for bribe or threat, but children too can develop a shrewd manipulative skill along the line used by Delilah to Samson: "If you really loved me . . ."

It is love which is the most powerful weapon in the armoury, and it is all too easy to hear the disguised blackmail in so many parent/teenager negotiations. The threats and promises of childhood echo in the noise of the teenage/parent skirmishes. The assurance of love has to stand unshaken behind the alarms. But that does not mean that the parent must not let his or her own vulnerability be seen.

It is so important to discover how to develop the mutual respect which will make the home a place where these natural clashes can be coped with and resolved.

For the midlife parent, the children may well produce anxiety and stress, but on the other hand, it should be possible to discover a way in which parents and their adult children can become good friends, and therefore a great source of mutual support and affection. The trusted teenager may be irritating in the extreme of his or her own exploration, and yet a solid rock in dealing with parental neuroses. It is one of the challenges of midlife to emerge as close, trusting and intimate friends with our children, which will stand us in good stead for the future stages of our lives.

At the same time as the midlife parents are going through this demanding process with their children, they may also be experiencing difficulties in their relationships with their own parents, who may be trying to cope with retirement or illness, and the loss of identity they can bring. Just as the midlifers are perhaps confused and doubtful about the purpose of their own lives, their parents may be faced with overwhelming changes and a frightening emptiness. If the parents have invested their whole selves in their work, their social environment and their home, they may have to come to terms with the loss of each of these extensions of themselves. The ageing process itself involves inevitable restrictions, reduction of opportunity and incapacity in life. It is quite likely that one of the older parents has died or is disabled, and there will often be depression and bereavement to cope with. All these things project onto the screen of the midlife person the very fears which may be making their own life so unstable. Just as they are facing the loss of their youthfulness, "going over the top", passing the halfway mark, so the elderly parent reflects the very fear which the midlife person feels. They present an image of the loss of power, the nearness of old age and, behind it all, the fear of death.

Retirement can be a great boon to all involved. It can open the way for people to do some of the things they have always wanted to do but never had time for. It can result in their having more time to be grandparents, and to give their midlife children relief, support and some time on their own. Retirement, however, can also be a sad experience of the vacuum left by change. It is important at this stage (and earlier) to think about old age. Where are the parents to live? What will happen if there is serious illness or gradual disability? The couple who are quite fit and independent at retirement may within a few years be unable to maintain their property, climb their stairs, drive their car or do their beloved garden. This is a difficult transition, seeming to involve the sacrifice of most of what has made life worth-while. It may well suit both the grandparents and the midlife parents to shelve the issue until life becomes impossible and action is forced upon them. They may all collude in evading the decisions, because ageing is one thing none of them really wants to tackle. What seemed an excellent arrangement in early retirement may become a source of protracted grief in old age. The independent strength which the grandparents gave slowly reduces, so that the midlife adults have to be prepared to recognize their increasing demands and see that in some way they now have to be parents to their parents.

So many emotional confusions can be involved in this process. We feel guilty because we're not doing enough, yet resentful because the demands seem too great. The midlife person can start to nag the elderly parents as though they were children, and yet in the depth of the personality they are still their mother and father. The elderly parents recognize this shift in power and, whilst they have to accept the enforced limitations, they will cling on to each shred of independence as long as they can. Although this can sometimes be infuriating to the younger generation, and even a real hazard, it is basically a sound instinct. The elderly who avoid continuing adult responsibility and revel in dependence happily lapse into being like a child in opting out and personally reducing their own identity.

It was Baroness Wootton who said "As we grow older we become more the people we are". This can be for good or ill, depending on what sort of person we have been. It is not only arteries which can harden, but also the negative and angry characteristics. This can lead to conflict and, in the most extreme cases, to bullying and complete breakdown in relationships. Although middle age is the time when most people have to be responsible for elderly parents, the midlife period is often the time when the very process begins, and may be the time when sensible planning for old age and its possible trials should be made.

Those stages often coincide with the time when teenage children, as I have suggested, are experiencing painful transition. The midlife parents can sometimes feel that they are trying to face in all directions, attempting to give advice which is consistently rejected, and to work out what is proper independence with young and old alike. At the same time, they may feel they have to spend a great deal of effort in caring maintenance about the home. The person in midlife wants a bit more time to him- or herself, perhaps to develop a new direction in a job, or a new creative pastime, or is desperate for a bit of time and space to work things out, when the door to freedom shuts again as new and complicated responsibilities develop.

It is my hope and belief that the generations can continue to be a tremendous help and encouragement to each other. It can be a time when the ageing grandparents have much to offer the midlife people, and vice versa. But it will depend upon mutual respect and allowing each other the space to make the best of their own particular stage. The ageing parent will have to accept that the midlife parents need to spread their wings and to express the freedom and responsibilities appropriate to their time of life. The midlife parent will have to find ways of maintaining a secure and loving environment for the ageing parents, yet giving them the space to preserve a proper independence.

At their heart, these are spiritual issues about ageing and facing up to each stage of life as it is offered to us, and I tackle this in the last chapter.

4

Loving into Middle Age

At the centre of many a midlife crisis is a search for love. We need love, and some of the most crazy things we do are a desperate attempt to find it. From the period of infancy through to old age, we are reaching out for someone to love and someone to love us. If we are secure in love, we can cope with almost anything, and if we are starved of it we hurt. Midlife is for many people a time of disturbance in their search for love. For the single person, it can feel like the last chance. For the married, it can be a time when the children are growing up and leaving home, necessitating a new focus for the couple who may have become stale with each other. The "threat" of middle age can cause anxiety about sexuality and intimate relationships.

So it is that many people break the pattern of life – looking for some greater fulfilment, discovering what they believe is a new, true romance which sets their adrenalin racing, makes them feel young again, opening up vistas of satisfaction, intimacy and affection which they have not yet experienced, or which have become things of the past.

The sexual needs shout louder as the person sees youth receding, and faces the downhill journey in the fear of sexual frustration, boredom and loneliness. These difficulties are serious, and failure to cope with them is widespread. This is not only demonstrated in the alarming divorce rate, but also in the way people who stay together allow the gulf between them to get wider and more despairing. In this chapter I shall try to say how I think we can be loving into middle age.

Sexual energies, attraction and activities, have been prevalent in the creation of God as long as there has been animal life on this planet, and our sexual behaviour and identity are a central fact of human experience. We are not the first permissive age; there have been many before us – and even if there had not, it is possible to show how even in more repressed societies, sexuality exercised considerable power over people's behaviour.

Contemporary Pressures

There are, however, features which in our contemporary society are relatively new and profoundly affect our thinking and our midlife experience. First, media propaganda and indoctrination; secondly, the belief that by using modern contraceptive techniques, fully expressed sexual relationships need not lead to pregnancy; and thirdly, the wider acceptance that homosexuality is a natural way of being for a minority of people.

Through advertising, television, videos and the printed word, we are exposed continuously to sexual images. Most often, the image is of the young man or woman, beautifully in their prime, enjoying the apparent freedom of an uninhibited, thoroughly satisfying, sexual adventure. Even if the adventure ends in disaster, divorce or violence, in some way this does not diffuse the glamour. These portraits convey two messages – first, sexual activity is extremely satisfying, and secondly, we all have a right to such satisfaction. Perhaps – as with televised football – we shall be sated by over-exposure! For most people, however, a sexual appetite is stimulated which will never be satisfied. We seem to ignore the fact that so often the media models themselves, who stimulate this appetite, go from unsatisfactory relationship to unsatisfactory relationship, living the deception which is being commercially exploited. It can be sobering to see the "celluloid" beauty ten years later in the flesh, cracked and wrinkled.

Sometimes I have sat in the home of a family where the husband has been out of work for years, and the television is on. As we talk, images of the affluent world flash before us – the Christmas gifts, the holidays in Spain, the hi-fi, stereo, video, new car of the year. The whole show is beyond his reach, it's as much as he can do to survive from one social security payment to the next, let alone consider a holiday or a computer for his children – whereas there is so much in human affection, understanding and comfort he can still offer. I think this is a parable of the experience of most people who are subjected to the propaganda that total sexual satisfaction is easily accessible. We see the images of the exciting and successful sexual encounter, but feel that in our present situation there can be no satisfaction – so a sense of frustration, loss and self-pity can be created. We may look like Laurel and Hardy, but expect to be Paul Newman and Robert Redford; we may build ourselves up to a marvellous experience, only to discover that it was just the same as last time; we may momentarily see some beauty in ourselves, yet the cold light of day shows we have more in common with Hilda Ogden than Bo Derek.

The propaganda can stimulate our sexual expectations, and undermine the sexual satisfaction which real life offers us. But the propaganda does not just cause dissatisfaction, it can also persuade us to get the sexual side of our lives out of proportion. Our own personal memory bank has so many sexual images imprinted that they can become a persistent playback. This can mean that grown, adult people become like adolescents, who for a period can think of little else than their sexual fulfilment. It can become a sort of addiction, which can only be fed by more images if physical satisfaction is not available. So sexuality can become, through indoctrination, the most important and incessantly demanding facet of life. "We have a great thing going"; "My husband never gave me orgasms like this." All these words convey the most painful criticism and judgements on our partners who, like us, have often struggled to be loving and understanding through thick and thin – and have offered trust, love, affection and companionship, even though we may not have achieved the exploding excitements of Lady Chatterley and Mr Mellors. So sexuality has the power, magnified by the propaganda machine, to become the dominant facet of our experience, taking to itself importance and authority quite inappropriate to the reality available to most people in their lives.

Under the influence of the propaganda, too, we can begin to think of ourselves as unable to control our sexuality, attributing too much power to it, as though we were helpless. If we add to this the enticement of forbidden fruit and the excitement of guilt, before we know where we are it is overwhelming and seems impossible to control by an act of will. Then we can lose the determination to stay with, support, love our partner and children.

At midlife these pressures can become the source of a crisis. Anxiety about loss of sexual energy, fear of the loss of physical attractiveness, the need for comfort in a hard, competitive world where we have too much responsibility or not enough job satisfaction, the hovering fear of the downhill slope, the growing belief that we have got ourselves all wrong – can add even further thrust and power to the propaganda, and thus build up out of all proportion the dissatisfaction and the need for alternative solutions. Our grandparents did not have to cope with this media explosion. Nor did they have to cope with the Pill. That's another way in which our view of sexuality has changed in our own time. As many people discover, it is not as foolproof as we tend to think, but for most people the act of sexual intercourse has been separated from the likelihood of conception. This has important implications. Even for those who do not agree with the Roman Catholic teaching on contraception, it is clear that a change of attitude has taken place. The availability of contraception has profoundly shaken our moral thinking about sexual relationships. So much of sexual morality was based upon the fact that ensuing pregnancy was always a possibility and, in more sustained relationships, a probability. Now we face the fact that most of us use contraception, and we are thankful that, in the vast majority of cases, it is successful.

This immediately offers to people alternatives which were previously prevented by the proper taboos which society had developed to try to ensure that children would not be born out of the security and bonding of marriage. Now there are many people who live together, either as an experiment in preparation for marriage, or as the way they fully express their own adult relationship, without the desire to enter permanent marriage. Many people engage in sexual relationships purely for pleasure. "We'll see if it works", "No long-term commitment", "We can both walk away." Contraception also offers to married people opportunities for sexual relationships outside their marriage without so much risk of discovery, or the complication of unwanted parenthood, or the social scandal of an adulterous pregnancy.

Inside or outside marriage, sexual satisfaction, pleasure, comfort and companionship appear to be sufficient reasons in themselves for having a sexual relationship – and, rather like skiing, it's assumed that increased skill and athleticism are an enjoyable end in themselves. For the single person, there are no ties and so the options are there for the finding and taking. For the married, it is possible that a disappointing and boring sex life, or even frustration, anger and hate built on seven, ten, fifteen years of misuse and failure, make alternatives appear very attractive. Both partners may be working and having a wide variety of relationships, and as a result alternative partners are more readily available. After all, we are not alone in searching for love.

It may be that we are highly flattered by the attention of someone younger than we are, who restores to us our own image of youthful vigour and attractiveness, and with whom we can find a fresh start, leaving our partner stranded and worn down by the unresolved relationship and a severely damaged ego, whilst we rediscover our lost youth, energy, vitality.

It's no good our pretending that this change, brought about in part by the use of contraception, has not happened, but it is essential for the Christian to say where faith in Christ leads him or her in this new tantalizing and seductive market place. We have to live in it and find ways of being which are more satisfying or more true to ourselves, or just plain morally right.

A third major change of attitude in recent years has been

the acceptance by a far wider public of homosexual relationships as being natural for a substantial minority of
people. I deal with the midlife implications of this later in
this chapter, after I have thought about the single and the
married relationships.

The Single Life

Much Christian teaching seems to assume that marriage is
the goal and the most likely state of life for all except those
who have decided to be celibate. This is, of course, far
from the truth. More and more people decide not to be
married and, in spite of the matchmaking agencies, many
people live the whole of their lives alone as single people.
In the United Kingdom in 1985, there were approximately
one million spare men! In spite of the fact that my own
experience of being single is second-hand since 1965, I
want to begin this section by thinking about the single
person, because, after all, that's where we all begin.

From the late teens, most men and women come under
pressure to have a partner or partners. Society still man-
ages to suggest that if a person has no close particular
personal relationships there must be something wrong. I
have talked with many people for whom this pressure has
been extreme, through the unconcealed disappointment of
their parents, or the subtle and not-so-subtle innuendos
they pick up from people they know. There seems to be a
considerable pressure to say that the single person is in
some way falling short of what it means to be human. So
there can be, by midlife, a growing sense of fear that she's
going to be on the shelf for ever, or he's become a bachelor
who is rather stuck in his ways. Perhaps this pressure is
lessening as more people are choosing the single life. There
are also many people who have been through marriages
which did not work. But in spite of these real changes, the
social pressure to marry remains. When Gail Sheehy
published her book in the United States, only five per cent
of American men over forty were unmarried, and only

about ten per cent of women in America never marry.

Part of the social pressure is, no doubt, the religious pressure. It would be difficult to disentangle the genesis of these pressures from their religious origin. There are the instructions given by God to Noah and his sons: "Be fruitful and increase, and fill the earth" (Genesis 9:1), and the words of the marriage service, where the preface states that marriage was ordained for the "increase of mankind according to the will of God". Religion has endorsed the importance of the procreation of children. The Christian religion has been quite clear that this procreation of children is the purpose of sexuality, and that sexual intercourse (how dated and bureaucratic that word looks!) should only take place within marriage – thus carrying the moral by-product that all unmarried people should remain celibate. Although the procreation of children remains important, we face a world where many countries are disastrously overpopulated, and many Churches would teach the positive value of contraception. The new emphasis has to be on population control. In spite of the Christian emphasis on marriage, there is also a high doctrine of celibacy – even sometimes suggesting that marriage is a second-best. St Paul wrote the following, under the impression that there was not long to go before the end of the world:

> To the unmarried and to widows I say this: it is a good thing if they stay as I am myself; but if they cannot control themselves, they should marry. Better be married than burn with vain desire.
>
> 1 Corinthians 7:8–9

It is also a fact that our Saviour was single, and there is no higher model of life than His. But though the teaching of the Church and the example of Jesus give a high profile to the life of celibacy, it seems to leave the single person caught between a vocation of celibacy which he or she may not have, or marriage which may be unsuitable or unobtainable.

These social and religious pressures, however, are only

fuel to the fire which often burns in single people through their own need. This self-doubt can reach crisis proportions in midlife. As the woman faces up to or experiences the menopause, and men and women see the opportunity to marry disappearing, the social scene can make it difficult to create opportunities for mixing and developing suitable relationships.

The self-doubt raises such questions as "Has it been a failure on my part because I was afraid of commitment?"; "Have I sacrificed myself to my career?"; "I've spent my life looking for the right person and maintained my moral standards – wouldn't it have been better if I'd taken the less perfect opportunities which came my way?"; "Am I just an unattractive person?"; "Am I losing the capacity to have children – even with an accelerated timetable of courtship and marriage?"; "When I'm old and alone, who will love me?" This can give rise to bitterness directed both at the opposite sex for rejecting them, and against life and people in general.

But although these are real pressures, many of the negative assumptions which some married people make about single people are untrue. There is much to affirm in being single, and we all know deeply fulfilled and happy single people. The stereotyping of the lonely, frustrated, cramped single person in midlife is absurd. There can obviously be pain and hurt and loneliness, but it is important to see the advantages, the strengths, the gifts of the single life.

For the person who believes he or she is called by God to the celibate life, the singleness is given an added sense of destiny. Although in their hearts there will be times of regret, grief, anxiety – nevertheless it is clear to them, and usually to the people around them in society, that they are single for a purpose which is holy and admirable within the life of the Christian Church. Such people, if they are priests or religious, or lay people who have made this decision, have exercised a free choice before God. They will often live in community with others who are committed to the same purpose. This is a tremendous further support and affirmation, although rumour has it that living in community can be hell.

I remember drawing a highly secular laugh from a large gathering of religious when I told the true story of a person who wanted to become a religious to get away from the pain and temptations of the world! The religious life can be, and often is, an intense struggle from which the rest of us draw strength, but in the end it is a matter of choice and destiny rewarded by the hard-won joys of the celibate life. Even so, midlife can be perilous for a celibate priest or a religious, and there are a number who leave their orders to start a totally new life-style – by getting married, or by an uncompromising plunge into "the world".

However, most single people are not convinced they are called to be celibate – nor that they could or should be a professional religious. They may have decided that marriage or "partnership" is not for them, or they may be just women- or men-in-waiting. They probably have no strong sense of vocation to be single, and it looks almost like an accident that they have never found such a partnership. The threat which seems to be posed by midlife may be for them a time when they make rash decisions, devaluing the purpose and content of their lives, or when they take and accept a further and more final step into singleness. They may find a way of looking at their present and their future which gives them a positive destiny and purpose – whether or not they are going to find a partner. It can be a time of retreat into further isolation, of wearing a thicker mask, or developing harmful, increasingly self-destructive patterns of life, or it can be a time of discovery of a new sense of release and freedom, purpose and satisfaction in living. As Philip Welsh has wisely said, the freedom of being single can be evaded too!

The great temptation is to make sure that you have so full a routine that you never need spend an evening on your own unless you want to. In other words, you never actually have to face up to being alone. All you have to do is join a couple of evening classes, become involved at the local church and wash your hair on Saturday nights. Before you know where you are, this routine which you have made to support yourself, becomes a prison that traps you. Life becomes predictable and inflexible. You become addicted to routine. You don't so much live as negotiate a timetable. Or, if you are a less orderly sort of person, you may live in a flurry of nose and tail arrangements.

It is strange how often married people look back wistfully on the freedom of being single, while the single are trying as hard as they can to give that freedom away.

The Single Person, pp.4–5

The single person has a freedom, but what is the freedom for? As so often in our lives, it is easier to describe what we want to be free *from*, and not nearly so easy to say what we want to be free *for*. I shall say something about the importance of this sense of finding the centre of ourselves in my last chapter.

As a married man, I want to affirm how much single people have to offer. However much a family lives a life of service, it must inevitably spend a heap of time on itself – its love and the development of each member. The single person also should spend time for him- or herself, but there should also be a greater space for some of the best bits of life which marriage can make more difficult. I have seen how the unmarried priest and deaconess or Christian lay person can live out the saying of Jesus to Peter:

"We here", Peter said, "have left everything to become your followers." Jesus said, "I tell you this: there is no one who has given up home, brothers or sisters, mother, father or children, or land, for my sake and for the Gospel, who will not receive in this age a hundred times as much – houses, brothers and sisters, mothers and children, and land – and persecutions besides; and in the age to come eternal life."

Mark 10:28–30

The nuclear family can easily become one of the most selfish manifestations of human life. The single person has the opportunity to belong to a wider family, a family where there is an enormous unmet need of love and affection, and who can return a great deal of them both.

There is not only a wider family, but also a chance of greater service. This could sound tedious, but the people who are most tedious are those who only care about, and look after, themselves. There is a beauty in the human being where he or she gives him- or herself to the service of people or a righteous cause, not for the avoidance of self and identity, but because the world works better where people give of their lives to others. In my experience, single people are able to play a unique role in the life of communities, and this can bring a high level of satisfaction and purpose. How many times have we seen bravery and self-sacrifice because a person "had only themselves to consider"? So, whereas singleness can be a most selfish way of life, like the man who buried his talent through fear – it can also be a source of marvellous strength, righteousness and love in the community in the steps of our single Master.

Singleness can also be affirmed in midlife because the single person should have more time and space to enjoy the beauty of the earth and creative leisure. We only have one life to lead. As Donald Nicholl points out in his excellent book *Holiness*, we can now extend our interests in so many ways that it can become a sort of greed for experience. The family is a complex unit in which to pursue individual interests, and there should be greater opportunity in single life to enjoy the theatres, the arts, the music, which most married people promise themselves one day they will do. To quote Philip Welsh again:

> Just as married people can misunderstand the single, so too the single can suffer from fantasies about marriage and become needlessly unhappy by dwelling enviously upon an idealized picture of married life that bears little relation to reality. It is a Christian principle not to waste yourself in fantasy about what you might have been, but to look for the fulfilment that God is offering you in what you are.

The Single Person, pp.3–4

One of the real difficulties of marriage is that it can mean we have little time for our friends. Obviously there are many lonely single people, and they must seize the opportunity of midlife to take positive, practical steps to find friends. Friendship is an art form. With good organization of time and priorities, the single person has an opportunity for deepened friendships which will hardly be possible for the married couple. It's only too easy for a married couple to get the idea that they both have to like each other's friends, and only to manage to meet their friends once in a blue moon, and then on over-organized occasions. The really successful single people I know, are those who have positively affirmed and lived to the full their membership of a wider family, their service to the community, their enjoyment of beauty and creative hobbies and, above all, the love of their friends.

It has been a cruel stereotype of some single people to say that they wasted the prime of their lives on their parents: the daughter who sacrificed her life to care for her mother or father, or the son who never got away from his mother's apron-strings (an interesting sexist differentiation). Although I do not believe parents have a right to expect one of their children to look after them in that way, nevertheless it does seem right if the child and the parent are still great friends and give each other mutual respect and support. I believe this relationship can be immensely worthwhile and a proper expression of midlife. The pain may come from being different generations, so that the child will be left when the parent dies. It is essential, therefore, that such a son or daughter has their own full life in their peer-group world. I know a man who nursed his mother through the difficulties of her senile dementia until she died. I have no doubt in my mind that his was a witness to the love at the heart of the universe and the purpose of all our human relationships. So I believe that a single person may well be able to give companionship, love and support, and receive it from a parent, as a most positive factor in their life, as long as they do not lose their friendships in their own generation as a result.

Marriage

What the Book of Common Prayer describes as "An honourable estate, instituted of God Himself", is going through difficult times. So great is the problem that every reader of this book will have friends or relatives who have been through serious difficulties in marriage, and separated. Many of the problems which used to be taken for granted and endured as part of "for better or worse", are now seen as reasons for giving up. It is not unusual to hear young people saying that they will never get married. The Church has tried, by her teaching and discipline, to stem this flood, but as any vicar or registrar knows, it already seems overwhelming.

For several years, I shared the work of a multi-disciplinary team of doctors, social workers and others, which provided a marriage self-help unit. We tried to offer a process of rebuilding marriage relationships. The doctors realized that many of the symptoms presented to them by patients were really caused by marital tension, frustration and worry, and these could not be dealt with properly in surgery hours. Sadly, many of the couples came to us when the hurt was already so sharp and ingrained that it proved impossible to achieve reconciliation and a new start. So much of my time as a priest has been spent in marriage counselling that I begin to wonder whether there are any straightforward happy marriages (besides mine, of course!).

In spite of rather gloomy evidence, I remain convinced that married life can be the source of the greatest joy in life, the most secure base for the bringing up of children and potentially the best way to share life together "till death us do part". I believe the Church has been right to stand up for this ideal, though it has meant incurring the anger of many. I want to help people find ways of saving their marriage if it is in difficulty, not encourage them to abandon it.

In many ways people do try to live together in accordance with an ideal pattern. The patterns will vary greatly in terms of the expectations of the partners, their own parents and society. But we usually fall short of our ideals. We would perhaps like to be fair, open-minded, tolerant, loyal, encouraging and filled with mutual respect and love. We would probably like our marriage to go on getting better and more happy, for our own sake and that of our children. But for many people this seems to be impossible. Husbands and wives often find themselves facing agonizing decisions. The wife who recognizes that her husband is never going to accept that she is an independent person – and has to make the choice between staying married or taking the opportunity to become a person in her own right. The husband who has been unable to communicate how frustrated and lonely he feels because of his wife's coldness. After sessions of listening to all the grief and the hurt, the counsellor often wonders how the marriages can possibly continue. On the other hand, many married couples seem to let their relationship drift into no more than co-existence. We all know people who have stayed together only to become permanent prosecutors of each other, sniping and scoring petty victories.

I have become convinced that a married couple not only have to be well prepared before they get married, but also every so often take time to re-evaluate how their relationship is progressing. There seems to be a great reluctance to evaluate our marriages, although the breakthrough of organizations like "Marriage Encounter" is an encouraging development. So many partners in married life only want to talk to their own, chosen, comforting outsider, and avoid the necessary discomfort of tackling the issues face to face with the only person who knows the relationship as well as they do, i.e. their husband or wife. Everyone agrees that good communication between husband and wife is essential – so much damage is done because the couple do not talk to each other – yet I am not saying that married couples can share everything in their minds. That has the ring of absolutist dogma, which itself can be hurtful and ride roughshod over the sensibilities.

From time to time it may seem to a wife or husband that her or his own fulfilment alone is the ultimate good, and therefore sufficient reason to abandon the marriage, but the Christian has to consider the ultimate good of the other people involved – not only the wife or husband and the grown children, but also the wife or husband of the possible new partner, and their children. There are a lot of people involved in this pursuit of personal satisfaction. Before deciding to make changes which can have such wide and maybe damaging effects, everything ought to be tried to enrich, restore, reinvigorate, re-create the existing relationship. They need to rediscover, if possible, the fun, physical relaxation, and affection. I am not advocating an impossible ideal, because I realize that for some the breach is so severe that there can be no going back, but I believe that for many, a new look at the relationship, a new honesty about hidden resentments, a new sharing of what gives pleasure, a new set of shared interests, a new way of looking at the individual and the partnership, can work miracles.

Patterns of behaviour and expectation in the marriage develop over the years to the stage when one partner reaches breaking point. He or she could scream, and probably does, that life is passing them by without fulfilment. They may feel that they are just being used by husband/wife/children/ parents – everyone. "It's unfair – I need some space to myself!" If this is not faced, it can result in the partners avoiding real communication, running away into work or activities or pleasures or material improvements or financial security or whatever – when the heart of the problem is a desperate and profound loneliness which can only be solved by opening up the communication again. Late-night television, activism, blatant personal funk, keep the couple apart, and help them avoid the necessary meeting of hearts and minds.

Their sexual relationship, its success or failure, can seem to become the key focus of the problem, and may indeed be a serious symptom. It is often the case, however, that the real cause is the permanent breakdown of communication which means that misunderstandings multiply, resentments fester on, rejections are never healed and the couple don't give themselves the chance to talk it all through, to progress via good communication into relaxed intimacy and love, and from there into fulfilling sexual expression. It is often as much a matter of sorting out the relationship hang-ups which will restore the sexual enjoyment as it is of sorting out the sexual hang-ups to restore the relationship. I can't trace who said intimacy without sex was far preferable to sex without intimacy, but they were right.

Most of us possess the capacity to have normally happy sexual relationships. It is essential to be able to talk, or at least be sensitive, about the experience. What is it that gives him/her pleasure? What is it that turns him/her off? What are we afraid of? What are we trying to prove? What do we fear might be proved? Many people are still shy about these things, and certainly my generation and the preceding generation have not found it easy to discuss them. The discovery of mutual pleasure is a perfectly proper aim of married life. Dissatisfaction, coldness and rejection over a long period, can send partners out to the pub for alcoholic comfort, or into the arms of someone else, who offers romance, and is not worn out by loads of washing and housework, or depressed by an unshaven, smelly husband, or a preoccupied, tense and sharp-edged wife.

Evaluation of the marriage relationship will therefore have to include a shared appraisal of the habitual patterns of intimacy or pretended intimacy of the marriage partnership. This reappraisal must be followed up by the necessary changes in attitude and practice.

It is also necessary to reassess the goals of the marriage. We were married with purposes in mind, which for some will have been those stated in the marriage service:

[Matrimony] was ordained for the procreation of children . . .
It was ordained for a remedy against sin, and to avoid fornication . . .

It was ordained for the mutual society, help and comfort, that the one ought to have of the other, both in prosperity and adversity.

Book of Common Prayer,
Solemnization of Matrimony

The wording of the second aim seems very negative, and I always think the third goal should be put first, but they still look pretty realistic. As a marriage progresses, however, it is important to look at its developing purposes and the aims within it. This will mean making sure that there is time to talk about the future, about the children and their plans, about the targets to be achieved, whether they are material and financial, or spiritual and relational. Marriages can get stuck, habits become prisons, and many opportunities for new life will be stifled if there is no proper sharing of positive aims. Sometimes a terrible illness or a death or an accident jolts partners into reappraising their marriage. A woman was dying of cancer at forty-five – her council house had been made like a palace, with every conceivable gadget and beautification. As she approached her death, her question was "What is it all for?" In another family, mum and dad saw their young daughter dying of leukaemia. The wife went on the bottle, the dad became totally isolated and embittered. They could find no way of comforting each other. It is a sad fact that we leave so much of this thinking about what life is for until there is some tragedy. But it is a proper question at all times, perhaps especially at times of happiness and well-being, which can so quickly and subtly change into self-centredness, materialism and greed. So the sharing of goals is important in married life, to discover how far the partnership is able to be of service, not just to their own family but to the community; to discover where each partner is in terms of their own character and personal identity; to share together the implications of what Jung called the "second journey" – from midlife onwards. By reviewing the "contract" as they move towards middle age, by getting back close to each other, by a better understanding of what the other wants, it is possible to begin that journey with the confidence that we can love into middle age and beyond.

"Fun" is another big word in the marriage relationship. I reckon that a sense of humour is often a manifestation of the image of God in us. I'm not talking about the hollow or mocking laughter which covers up despair, and which can be evasion of the necessary turning to face reality and making an opportunity for healing and resolution. We can soon lose the sense of fun when the child in each one of us is totally submerged as our responsibilities grow and drag us down, or threaten to make us take ourselves too seriously. The delightful and helpful book by Thomas Harris called *I'm O.K. – You're O.K.* has wise things to say about people who kill off the child in themselves. If the grown-up in us becomes so dominant that we must always be managing other people, sermonizing them, controlling and rebuking them, then we become a menace and will find it difficult to have a proper sense of fun. Some marriage relationships somehow demand that one partner is always the parent and the other the child in their mutual reactions. This is damaging for both. It's damaging for the "parent-type" partner, because he or she is forced into the position of being the person who agonizes about decisions, who always has to take responsibility and who finds it difficult to see what their partner and children find so funny about salt in the sugar bowl. It is also damaging for the partner who is repeatedly the child in the partnership, evading the decisions, permanently acting the clown, and quietly retreating into habitual regression. Both partners need to act as parent and as child, both partners need to share responsibility, agonizing and decision-making, and both partners need to be able to let their hair down, do some clowning, enjoy a bit of whole-hearted irresponsibility. Fun based on a sharing of the adult and the child in each of us is a wholesome and necessary part of the survival kit – often ignored by those who are addicted to being bossy without the leaven of humour. Children and grandchildren should provide a wonderful opportunity and reminder that the child in each of us is treasured by God and holy:

> Truly I say to you, unless you turn round and become like children, you will never enter the kingdom of heaven.
> Matthew 18:3

A marriage also thrives on its capacity to look beyond itself. A couple who grow into old age without thinking much of anyone else but themselves and their children, are a warning sign. When all the carpets have been replaced, every possible alteration and extension made to the house, all the worn-out things discarded in favour of the new or the antique, the television is turned on – and then where are they heading? If the home and the family have become the only expression of the partnership, eventually it will lead to a vacuum. There has to be an outgoing, unselfish expression of the marriage, if it is to be whole.

A married couple who simply concentrate on themselves – their home, their family, their leisure – are basically spending their lives in self-service. I would claim that this is not only bad for individual partners, but also bad for the marriage and bad for society. For those who follow this way, it becomes increasingly necessary to protect their own standard of living at all costs. They learn to live in their own narrow world, their own comfortable home, and play no part in the vocation we all have to work for the betterment of society, or care for its members. The world we live in is full of suffering, both in the poorer nations and also in the poor and damaged of our own villages, towns and cities. People suffer just around the corner, as well as in the starvation belt.

Not only is there desperate suffering to be tackled, but also there is a necessary struggle to mend the profound damage done by evil and to work for a better world. It has certainly not been proved that increased affluence in a nation makes for less crime and less personal hurt! The violence and the lack of direction amongst young people reflect attitudes of society which they see demonstrated before them. We cannot isolate football hooliganism, thieving, sexual abuse, the drug culture, from the family and the family culture which we have allowed to become the norm. We often speak of the damage done by broken marriages, which can indeed be a huge factor in any moral disintegration of the children involved – but I believe it must also be said that much of the amorality comes from the basic selfishness of many marriages and much of our family life. So often the middle-aged people condemn our young for what is only the logical extension of our own self-centred priorities and agendas. This can be rampant materialism, or a gross self-service which leaves children, as they grow towards adult life, without any sense of service to the community or to the poor, to the damaged or to the lonely. It can also leave them with their need for idealism so frustrated that they have to find their satisfaction in other ways to fill up the great spiritual vacuum they have inherited. Jesus said:

> Where your treasure is, there will your heart be also.
>
> Matthew 6:21

Hearts invested in things will end up empty.

There is much in the Christian faith which can provide a warning against this egocentricity of a marriage. It is part of the teaching of Jesus that our way of life, if it is to bring us fulfilment, will involve self-giving. If there is to be happiness, then there has to be the generous sacrificial, external side to a family's life:

> Anyone who wishes to be a follower of mine must leave self behind; he must take up his cross and come with me. Whoever cares for his own safety is lost; but if a man will let himself be lost for my sake and for the Gospel, that man is safe. What does a man gain by winning the whole world at the cost of his true self?
>
> Mark 8:34–36

That is not just a call to an individual discipleship, but it is a call to a Christian family. It is a warning that self-absorbed family life, and a self-absorbed marriage, sacrifice the true selves and potential of the people involved. But why should we bother? Why should we care for others, and why should there be this outgoing dimension to a family's life? The person who believes in God may say it is because God has shown us that it is the way to live, the way to happiness. Jesus, who was above all a self-giving person, said:

> I am the way; I am the truth and I am the life . . .
>
> John 14:6

Those of us who believe in God should see our lives as being on loan from God, and there is a profound responsibility in this human "being". But this is not just the demand of a righteous God, it is also His offer to us of the true self, of real identity, of "abundant life":

> The Law of the Lord is perfect and revives the soul.
>
> Psalm 19:7

Quite often, it will seem old-fashioned, or "do-goodish", or "holier-than-thou" to be a family which takes seriously the service of the community or our neighbours, but I firmly believe that to live in an egocentric circle is the way to emptiness, to inner despair, however much it may appear to be clothed in success. There is in Psalm 73 an accurate picture of how it can feel to take on a more God-loving, self-giving life-style in a materialistic, affluent society. The psalmist expresses his envy of the people who have been totally egocentric:

> No pain, no suffering is theirs;
> they are sleek and sound in limb;
> they are not plunged in trouble as other men are . . .
> Therefore pride is their collar of jewels . . .
>
> Psalm 73:4–6

He was puzzled by this problem that those who do not set

themselves the tasks of the goodness of God seem to prosper, and those who care for the poor suffer torment. He says that he almost gave in:

> My feet had almost slipped,
> my foothold had all but given way,
> . . . I found it too hard for me,
> until . . .
>
> Psalm 73:2,16,17

Until what?

> . . . until I went into God's sacred courts;
> there I saw clearly what their end would be.
>
> Psalm 73:17

There is often this rather unattractive self-righteous element in the psalms, but the great point which I take from these verses is that in the worship of God, and in prayer, we can come to see things quite differently. We can learn to put a different value on all facets of life. The worship of God is not only important and beautiful for us, because through it we express our love for God and sense His love for us, but also because under its influence we can learn to see what God wants us to be.

This challenges our marriage and family life, especially in our affluent generation. The multiple dangers of our world, above all the nuclear threat, will make us question again what life is for and what are the truly valuable experiences, which best express our freedom. For me, the whole of this vision depends upon the reality of God, and the vision of life which loving Him and being loved by Him gives. It is for those who hold secular creeds to argue how this vision grows for them. Erik Erikson describes this outgoing experience as "generativity":

> Generativity means feeling a voluntary obligation to care for others in the broadest sense. Having children does not

ensure generativity, nor does being childless necessarily prevent it . . . Adults who miss out on the enrichment of generativity . . . will lapse into prolonged stagnation.

Quoted in Sheehy, p.405

I am often impressed at the emergence of the unselfish life-style amongst people who say they have no God – I can only rejoice and marvel in that. At the same time I recognize that for myself the sense of responsibility draws its strength from my encounter with God. To put it another way, I seem to be closer to God, both as an individual and with others, when trying to exercise responsibility, not only to my own family, but also for people who are not of my tribe. I do not say that there is no moral sense without belief in God, no morality without religion, but I do believe that God is the source of the moral vision of all people.

I have discussed at some length this question of the external self-giving dimension of a marriage partnership because I think it is a part of the key to midlife and the journey into middle age. At this stage of life, when people usually enjoy greater material security, we can either go up the spiritual cul-de-sac of an egocentric marriage, or recognize and embrace the possibility of a more generous life-style. Until then, it may have been more difficult, as we try to survive babies, caring for young children, starting a home and build-ing up our job – all of which can make an overwhelming agenda. Then the visible priorities we choose in midlife will undoubtedly affect our children, and either help them discover a spiritual sense of direction, or lose them in the fog of unbridled selfishness.

It is not surprising that we find marriage difficult. It is a solemn undertaking to offer yourself to another person for life and take them on in return. The whole unity implied in "The two shall become one flesh" is profound and so much more than just a physical union. The unity is vital, but at the same time the two people also remain individuals. Marriage is a partnership, not a take-over bid. Each partner has their own identity, their own needs, their own spiritual characteristics.

So often marriage is seen as a way of extending one personality and agenda wholesale onto another. The good communication depends upon the two people themselves developing their own identity, their sense of personhood and proper independence. Both partners will need the space and friendships necessary to be fully themselves. Domination, ownership, subjugation of emotions and intellect, don't just damage the victim, they also damage the oppressor. Marriage should be a relationship between two distinct people, with their own individuality and combination of strength and weakness.

For instance, it cannot be assumed that the partners will believe the same things. In the Church, we often see the division which is caused by one partner being a Christian and the other not. It is only one example of where, in ideological terms, there are sharp differences of belief and practice. This is obviously not just the problem of religious people, but for everyone it spreads out into the whole question of values and attitudes. A husband may think that work is the be-all and end-all of existence, where his partner may think of work as being simply a means to an end. A wife may believe strongly in a compassionate society, whereas her husband may be fiercely committed to the competitive society and the survival of the fittest. It may be that the husband believes in the children being given maximum freedom and independence, when the mother believes children grow up far too quickly, and need the learning of restraint and discipline.

The beliefs of the partners in a marriage, if they are taken seriously, can lead to considerable tension which can build up in midlife and afterwards. I have spoken already of the necessity for two real, personal, distinct identities, and nowhere is this more important than in what partners believe. It is often the case that one partner holds or expresses belief in stronger terms than the other, and therefore there can be a tendency for that view to become the dominating ideology of the partnership. There has, therefore, to be a proper mutual respect for each other's views. It is hoped that there would already be much in common, because the two people got on well enough to be married in the first place, but it needs working on all the way through. When one partner uses emotional blackmail, or bullying tactics, to develop a sort of censorship on the other, real damage is being done to both. It's yet another good reason for the slow preparation for marriage which takes full account of the way both partners look at life, as well as the way they look at each other. So there has to be good communication – listening and speaking to find the way through for two distinct identities trying to be one unit.

This in part lies behind the anxiety caused by the desire to promise "to obey" in the wedding service. In the end, supremacy is then given to the husband, and if there is a profound disagreement, he has the right and duty to decide. But most people now cannot agree to a marital hierarchy, and do not wish to begin their married life with shared perjury! But if we do not have a clear hierarchy and supremacy, then we have to be careful to recognize that we don't reintroduce supremacy in all sorts of other ways – by control of the bank account, by intellectual agility, by emotional blackmail. The aim is to have the two partners using their own identity to find their common goals and to make their decisions together. This requires a high degree of tolerance, mutual respect and honour. Earlier my wife would not tell me how she voted at General Elections because she felt I might put undue emotional pressure on her. Every election, I had to live with the uncertainty that she might cancel me out! She felt unsure about her own political identity, and bullied by mine. As she became more sure of what she believed, she felt able to argue it out. If midlife is to be another step towards maturity of soul, then both partners have to go on growing and discovering the truth for them, both within their own identity and in their combined operation.

This is especially important in the development of faith. Faith is not something which you can rely on your partner to have for you. One of the saddest facets of a vicar's time spent visiting homes to talk to people about faith is caricatured with too much accuracy by the man who comes to the door, sees

the dog-collar and says, "Ah, you want to see the wife."
Religion, children, personal relationships are, in some parts
of society, women's business. It's almost as though the men
think you can have faith and personal understanding vicar-
iously – rather in the same way that some women expect the
family car to run without being filled up with petrol, or the
roof gutters to be kept in good repair without a ladder.
Obviously in a marriage there will be an allocation of areas of
responsibility, as in any sensible organization, but ideas,
faith, values, cannot be delegated. Our soul is our own soul,
and we are responsible for it.

Married couples are often temperamentally very different,
so they will respond to faith and values in different ways. We
must not expect our partner to be a sort of clone of what we
ourselves are. One may be a river flowing quietly through the
plain, whereas the other may be turbulent, like the rapids.
One may be a rather unexpressive and calm solid person, and
the other may be extrovert and noisy in their opinions. The
key is for both to have the opportunity to be themselves and
develop within the marriage as fully as they can develop – not
just into a poor copy of their partner. We cannot leave prayer
to our partner, nor worship, nor thinking it out, nor
deciding, nor believing. If a marriage settles into a pattern
where the beliefs of one dominate, and are then assumed to
be the beliefs of the partnership, there is the raw material for
midlife crisis, middle-age resentment and destructive non-
communication in old age. The success of the partnership
depends upon the health and strength of both identities.

In the next chapter I shall be tackling the changing role of
men and women in society, but at this point I want to look at
some of the personal implications of these changes for the
marriage relationship.

When my wife first went out to work, I was interested that
I felt miserable if I was home by five-thirty and she was not
there. I was saying to myself, "I've done a day's work and still
have an evening meeting, and visits to make, and here I am
having to get the tea." I thought of the men I had heard in the
marriage guidance sessions who were so offended that their

wife was not there to put their slippers out, to bathe their wounds and lay on the comfort of a meal. "She didn't ever have my tea ready" was a constant cry. I began to realize that the need I and they were expressing was really a mother-need. I had been used to the comfort of a welcoming mother as a child. It was good and helpful to me, and, in a way, I suppose I was addicted. It is natural in some ways that husbands expect some mothering by their wives, just as some wives expect some fathering from their husbands. I like the story of the man who put a fork through his foot and came limping into the kitchen. His wife appeared in her most seductive negligee – it was not the wife he wanted at that moment. In a way, it is easy to caricature this infantile desire in adults, but it is surprisingly powerful, and is a factor to be dealt with when the woman changes to a working or socially active role. The expectations of husband and children are threatened, and some honest talk and adjustment will be necessary. I have seen men go into a permanent sulk because they do not have the mother-comfort they have been programmed to expect.

The difficulties can go far beyond this rather primitive need of mothering. The man may build his manliness on his being the bread-winner, on his masculine struggle in the hard, rough world. Suddenly, he can find that his wife is tackling the same issues and doing the job better. He may depend on her being a dependent *Hausfrau*, and he may find this new, lively, decisive person a considerable threat to his own image of himself. Perhaps he is older than she is, and when they married he was definitely the more mature and the stronger character. Now, he sees his wife becoming very much a person in her own right, and he feels unsettled and, in a funny way, diminished. If she has work and he doesn't, it may be a most tremendous blow to his self-respect because of his expectation of himself as father and bread-winner.

I have witnessed many couples where this whole change has brought about a crisis leading to a separation, or to continuous rows, or to alcoholism, because the husband feels he has to find his comfort somewhere. Very often the couple's expectations have largely been modelled on their own parents' marriages, and they will carry inside themselves strong drives to repeat the pattern or fight it, rather than learn from it and move on. There is sometimes a ruthlessness in women at this point, which not only fails to recognize how much their husbands fear these changes, but then goes even further and uses the situation to defeat their man and punish him for previous oppression. I have seen women work to get their husbands reduced to nothing, and even evicted from their homes, whilst they start new relationships which are more in harmony with their emancipated selves. If the injustice is pointed out to them, they have at times said that it is only the same injustice committed by their husbands to them in the first place. These are not extreme cases, but reflect what is a form of the battle of the sexes, and it is a battle that, as a society, we have by no means negotiated with safety, without sometimes endangering the family stability so necessary to the secure upbringing of children.

There are Christians and, indeed, members of other faiths, who, recognizing this possible source of upheaval, simply withdraw into the pattern offered by the past. Both husband and wife then choose to operate within the headship of the male. This may be the safest and best way for them, but will be increasingly difficult to sustain if it is not a "contract" acceptable by both. The crisis can be seen at its most obvious when, for instance, Muslims living in the United Kingdom experience a challenge to their authority because their wives and daughters encounter the different mores of British education.

In the Bible, the headship of the male in the marriage partnership is clear, but it carries with it a strong doctrine of mutual respect and responsibility. The first subjection is of both husband and wife to Christ. In other words, because they are both obedient to the Spirit of Christ, then the partnership is on a strong foundation:

Be subject to one another out of reverence for Christ.

Ephesians 5:21

Then it continues:

> Wives, be subject to your husbands as to the Lord; for the man is the head of the woman, just as Christ is also head of the Church. . . . just as the Church is subject to Christ, so must women be to their husbands in everything.

> Husbands, love your wives, as Christ also loved the Church and gave himself up for it . . . In the same way men also are bound to love their wives as they love their own bodies . . .

> *Ephesians 5:22–28*

For many Christians now, however, the headship of the male does not accurately express the nature of the partnership in their marriage. There must be mutual reverence and honour, but decisions have to be made together and, though male and female contribute distinctive qualities and attitudes, they will not assume an ex-officio male supremacy. There is still a recognition that both partners are subject to God – if both are believers, and in their marriage they are equals. Obviously there are many ways in which one partner can dominate the other – by character or economics or emotional blackmail – but for many of us the "obedience" factor, wife to husband, has now been omitted from the contract. This choice has sometimes been made in the head, but not yet accepted in the heart – so that the volcano can go on being active long after both have accepted that it is, in theory, dead.

Thinking it out together can help. If a family is happily enjoying the fruits of mum working, then perhaps they will be able to take on a share of responsibilities which were traditionally mum's without too much resentment. There can be other positive gains, as in the sharing of parenthood, with dad being quite proud of his cooking, and certainly not threatened by pushing the pram through the streets. If his masculinity is threatened to such an extent that he loses confidence and feels impotent, then that will be bad news for both wife and husband. He will have to rediscover his own confidence by his own greater understanding, but perhaps it is also all the more reason for the wife to affirm and encourage him. If it can be seen that the new arrangement will be helpful to them both, and will give them better opportunities to be together, to enjoy a little privacy and rely on each other more, then perhaps the whole relationship will be strengthened. Care has to be taken about bringing home the worry and stress of two jobs, or living with the stress of no job. I have sometimes wondered whether people have quite realized how risky it is to have two whole sets of responsibilities, especially if both are highly demanding and produce anxiety. Husbands and wives have always had to cope with the difficulty of his coming home from work worried about the new boss, the old machine, etc., and his wife wanting to talk about the baby's wind or the baby's lack of wind, or the fight their child had with the next-door neighbour's little monster. It is a common failing in marriage that we don't really take it in turns to listen and support. I've known so many men who expect to pour out all their anxiety because they think their job is really important, and then will not listen to their partner's worries – "Can't you see I've had enough?" But the self-giving love of listening and supporting becomes more demanding, and even more necessary, if a marriage is trying to cope with two jobs.

It is my belief that our new understanding can be a great enrichment of the marriage, but that we often under-estimate the force of the subterranean non-rational energy which this disturbing change brings about. The use of the word "contract", because of its rather hard quality, reminds us that the covenant between a man and a woman in marriage is based on love, but is often expressed through very down-to-earth realities such as bank accounts, domestic arrangements, and shared responsibility for the home. The contract may be fixed and final in the nature of the original promise, but its physical, spiritual, material and social expression will often change sharply. Gail Sheehy says:

The couple contract must be renegotiated in midlife. That doesn't mean that two people sit down as if in a boardroom and hammer out a new deal overnight. It means that a series of readjustments must be made over a period of years. If this isn't done, she may well turn into just the domineering harridan he dreads – Big Mom, sworn somehow to even the score by becoming house-bursar and the curator of her husband's every weakness – while he perhaps slips into the passive and effeminized role of a Dagwood Bumstead.

Sheehy, p.422

"If you work every day, then I'll do the shopping, you do the ironing, we'll both do the garden, we'll have a joint bank account, you have your bank account – I'll look after the car and the outside of the house, you look after the inside." In this way, the benefits and disadvantages are shared, and there will not be the deep sense of injustice which often bedevils the less flexible approach to marriage relationships. Most of the marriages I know well – including my own – have experienced stress until the fair solution is found.

The sooner it ceases to be a fight to win and becomes a team effort, the better, allowing the man to be a man and the woman to be a woman in partnership.

Because the marriage partnership often undergoes the pressures I have so far described, an affair will sometimes appear an attractive release. It is an option which brings stress, whether it is refused or accepted. The possibility itself can bring a feeling of panic, instability and painful divided loyalties. Not only are there obligations to spouse and family, but also – for those who believe in God – it is against God's law. The husband or wife may be clear that there should be no affair – that the marriage must be saved – but the desire for this other love can be an impulsion which seems so much more powerful. Perhaps he or she makes the decision to stick by the marriage, and the moral energy is found to carry out the decision. It is still not simple. So often, the most painful moral choices are presented as if, once the decision is made,

73

all will be well. In reality, the pain of such a sacrifice can go on grumbling for many years. Like an old war-wound, under certain circumstances it can hurt. The difficulty about the sacrifices we make in our lives is that we often feel the need to punish someone else for the fact that we had to make them. In a marriage, the obvious person to blame for our having made the sacrifice is our partner. "If it hadn't been for you, I would have . . . " After repeated sexual failure or dissatisfaction, the fantasy of the perfect alternative comes to the mind and creates an even deeper anger. The anger and resentment are difficult to conceal – especially in bed – but also, in the normal to and fro of married life, the tone can so easily become resentful and punitive. In this way, the moral sacrifice becomes a further threat to the marriage it was made to save. It may be that the partner knows nothing of the temptation, has no idea about the source of the resentment, and therefore can do nothing to alleviate the situation. If it is not possible to talk about what has happened, then the responsibility for coping has to be carried alone, unless there is an important, totally trustworthy person with whom it can be shared and off-loaded.

In order to cope with the pain of such a sacrifice, there are steps to take which can alleviate the stress. It is important not to get addicted to suffering sacrificially. Having once made a self-denying decision of that magnitude, it is only too simple to keep on getting into the fixed position of the hard-done-by. Such a sacrifice does not make a martyr, and it is important to recognize that the need arose, not just out of the chemistry of potential lovers, but also because some real need was not being fulfilled in the marriage. It may appear that the sacrifice is all on one side, but there will probably have been plenty on the other. The priority, therefore, becomes to try to explore what is going wrong. What is it in the marriage that creates the feeling of deprivation? Has this been talked through together? What is wrong with the existing contract, and in what ways is it unfair? It may not be possible to say anything about the affair, but at least the fact that it happened or nearly happened must lead to a reform of the marriage. It may be that the whole relationship has gone stale. Maybe romance has gone; maybe child-rearing has made one partner a nagger, or work has made the other a bore. At least the potential affair shows that there is still life, and that life has to find expression within the marriage in which the commitment was "till death do us part". It will often be the case that the temptation to an affair has not just been to do with sexual frustration, but is more to do with the way a person is treated: "She finds me interesting"; "He is so thoughtful"; "We have so much to talk about"; "It's marvellous to feel like a person in my own right." Many of these needs may have much more to do with the people the partners have become in their marriage. Perhaps the pattern has pushed them into one sort of mould, and there is a cry for help. It is important to try to strengthen and expand the sense of personal identity, and this must be worked at by both partners in the marriage. It may be that the wife can take further steps towards making her own distinctive contribution to society when the children have become more independent. There can be a harrowing claustrophobia in marriage, and it may be that both partners need some space or more chance to have a social life outside the marriage. Many women are forced to see their whole self-expression through the channel provided by their husband's social contacts. The temptation to have an affair probably means that alterations have to be made in the pattern of the marriage, by achieving greater equality, finding ways of improving communication, and developing and enriching sexual intimacy.

The other main resource in tackling the pain of giving up a possible affair is praying. God wants our fulfilment and the development of our true self. That "true self" which we search for is not just of our own making – it grows out of the love of God. Prayer can "fill up our senses" and operate in us at the inner level where our identity is made or broken. If Jesus has revealed to us the whole nature of God, then in the self-giving we are going to discover the love of God. His sacrifice for us has helped to lift off our shoulders the burden of our countless failures – our debt to God is so huge, yet He loves us. We are primarily forgiven people. That is, we live free and hopeful because we are not bowed low by the hurt we do to ourselves and to others. So in spiritual terms, the sacrifice we make in the name of the love of our partner is a small part of God's creative love in the world. In a real sense, it is taking up the cross, joining in the sacrifice, sharing in the love and forgiveness of God. We can forgive ourselves for not taking the opportunity for self-fulfilment the affair promised to provide, we can forgive our partner for being the reason we made the sacrifice. This is not an easy prayer – nor a comfortable process. It will often involve desperate loneliness and probably anger at God and everyone – but it is a way.

It is hard to come back from the moral decision not to have an affair, but it is many times harder to come back from an affair itself. That is another good reason for finding the moral energy to resist it in the first place. The experience and information recorded on our mental and emotional tape by an actual involvement is so much more powerful than the temptation to have one. How can anyone find a way back? It is a process which has to be lived through – either alone, where it has been a secret, or with the partner.

I used to believe that there should be nothing held back between partners, but I have seen the additional damage done by an unfaithful partner's desire to tell all. Sometimes such penitence has to be carried within ourselves, when to share it would only do further harm. But in such a situation it would be essential to talk to a trusted person about it, because if there is no escape valve the pressure will build up and cause all sorts of subterranean feelings and confusion. The value of confession is that it makes us take our own wickedness seriously, provides a more objective and loving response, and can free us from the permanent trap of excessive guilt. But it is no use having a safe place to off-load our own failures if we are not at the same time taking the necessary personal steps to prevent repetition and to deepen and hallow the marriage.

The impact of an affair upon a marriage often involves

unexpected twists. The most common and overwhelming feeling is the partner's sense of rejection: "Something must be wrong with me if my partner needed to find satisfaction elsewhere." Although it may be dressed up in anger, it is often a profound sense of humiliation and staining which is directed inwards against the offended self. It is rather like the sense of guilt which is often experienced by a woman who has been raped. Also, the deception involved in the affair raises all sorts of questions about whether there can ever be trust in the relationship again. If it is a complete shock, then in one sense it's worse, because it throws doubt upon all the perceptions the faithful partner had of the marriage. This combines with the persistent fear that it might happen again – in spite of all the protestations of penitence and determination never to repeat the experience. Suspicion has been created, and it can act like a persistent, nagging doubt which takes away the trust which should be being re-created. There is a grieving which has to be lived through. There will probably be a need to put the unfaithful partner on the rack over and over again to exorcize the pain of the betrayal. Like bereavement, the process of grief will often go on much longer than seems fair to everyone else, especially to the partner who has tried to leave the affair behind. But, like bereavement, there does come a time when the injured partner has to start to share full responsibility for the renewed partnership and begin to cope themselves with any remaining grief and suspicion. It must not linger for ever as evidence for the prosecution, leaving the relationship with a totally unhelpful weight of guilt constantly creating a sense of obligation. Such a bias against the unfaithful partner, in the long run, will create patterns in the relationship which will undermine any new fairness and equality which will be necessary for restoration of the kind of love which makes marriage successful. It may well be that outside help will be needed to try to stand alongside the couple as they cope with this trauma.

There are spiritual elements in this process which are part of the healing process. The first and most important is forgiveness. As Christians, we are a forgiven people. That is to say, at the heart of our faith and experience there is our realization that we need to be forgiven. This is what makes Christianity so difficult for some people to accept. The gospels are full of stories which make the point that God forgives us for our many failings, and this releases in us the strength and grace to forgive others. St Luke relished this aspect of Jesus' teaching. The parable of the prodigal son tells of an elder brother who resents the love and forgiveness poured out on his erring but penitent brother. Jesus seems to have been far more critical of the self-righteous than of the penitent sinner. St Luke also invests much in the encounter between Jesus and the woman who lived an immoral life in the town. It is a beautiful, lived-out parable of our condition as human beings, both our self-righteousness and our sense of inadequacy and guilt.

A woman who was living an immoral life in the town had learned that Jesus was at table in the Pharisee's house and had brought oil of myrrh in a small flask. She took her place behind him, by his feet, weeping. His feet were wetted by her tears and she wiped them with her hair, kissing them and anointing them with the myrrh. When his host the Pharisee saw this he said to himself, "If this fellow were a real prophet, he would know who this woman is that touches him, and what sort of woman she is, a sinner." Jesus took him up and said, "Simon, I have something to say to you." "Speak on, Master", said he. "Two men were in debt to a money-lender: one owed him five hundred silver pieces, the other fifty. As neither had anything to pay with he let them both off. Now, which will love him most?" Simon replied, "I should think the one that was let off most." "You are right", said Jesus. Then turning to the woman, he said to Simon, "You see this woman? I came to your house: you provided no water for my feet; but this woman has made my feet wet with her tears and wiped them with her hair. You gave me no kiss, but she has been kissing my feet ever since I came in. You did not anoint my head with oil; but she has anointed my feet with myrrh. And so, I tell you, her great love proves that her many sins have been forgiven; where little has been forgiven, little love is shown." Then he said to her, "Your sins are forgiven."

Luke 7:37–48

There are few more impenetrable attitudes than self-righteousness. It is a natural defence employed by human beings, and it sometimes needs a supernatural grace to shift. When you have to listen to the stories of divorcees, it is sad how often self-righteousness has taken over. The language of the "guilty" and "innocent" party can sometimes express the reality, because individuals do do desperately wicked things to each other, but it is often a dangerous inaccuracy reinforced by the legal necessity to apportion blame. This becomes crystal clear when an "innocent" divorcee remarries and makes all the same mistakes, repeats the same patterns. When we think of ourselves as innocent, we want to beware as much as we need to beware when we feel too guilty. Jesus' words about specks and planks could provide an excellent motto for marriage:

Why do you look at the speck of sawdust in your brother's eye, with never a thought for the great plank in your own? How can you say to your brother, "My dear brother, let me take the speck out of your eye", when you are blind to the plank in your own? You hypocrite! First take the plank out of your own eye, and then you will see clearly to take the speck out of your brother's.

Luke 6:41–42

It is clear that self-righteousness is in itself an unhappy state. It separates us from others, puts us into a situation where we can feel superior and value ourselves more highly than we ought. To love God is to realize that we all fall short, and therefore are all in need of God's forgiveness.

To emerge from self-righteousness and to be able to forgive and be forgiven is the way to wholeness and maturity. Jesus offered this as a great blessing:

> Pass no judgement, and you will not be judged; do not condemn, and you will not be condemned; acquit, and you will be acquitted; give, and gifts will be given to you. Good measure, pressed down, shaken together, and running over, will be poured into your lap; for whatever measure you deal out to others will be dealt to you in return.
>
> Luke 6:37–38

This forgiveness in marriage is no easy movement of the heart, because we need love so badly that rejection at this level is a deep wound. But the discovery of forgiveness will be a freeing and enriching experience, and can open the way to renewed trust and tenderness, necessary if reconciliation is to be achieved.

It is not only forgiveness which is required for the healing and reconciling process, but also the restoration or building of a better self-image. When one partner has an affair, in the long run it will damage the self-image of them both. For the one, there is the sense of shame that he or she was able to do such a thing. For the other, there is the staining combined with the feeling of not being attractive, or interesting enough, or worthwhile, of being inadequate in the marriage. It may be that this low self-image will only serve to confirm a whole range of other such feelings – because of being absorbed in the home and the children, or because of a general sense of worthlessness. This sense of unworthiness, the look in the mirror that sees a dowdy, uninteresting, unattractive person, can become a matter of despair when the partner proves the image to be true by going off with someone else. This sense of inadequacy is so common throughout our experience, and is the cause of so many failed relationships and so much unhappiness.

It is especially prevalent in midlife, although a recurring

facet of most of our lives. The self-image has to be restored if the self-dislike and tendency to self-destruction are not to develop into more ingrained attitudes. This is why affirmation, self-acceptance and experiences which bolster our morale are so important. This mutual affirmation should be a constant source of comfort that "the one ought to have of the other", yet married couples so often get into the bind that they never do affirm each other. For instance, any idea that the one partner has, is instantly rejected as ridiculous by the other. So great is the inner resentment and antagonism, that even the positive gestures – the gift of flowers, the praise for an offer of help – are turned round and become a new stick to beat the other with. It is a sad fact that many married couples get into this reducing pattern of behaviour, and it can become a hundred times worse if behind it all lies a source of resentment, of sexual frustration, and a despair about the self. Again this is a central part of the Christian Gospel, because in that place where all our secrets are known, where we think we are pretty nearly unsavable, inadequate and maybe even loathsome, the love of God can come to bring assurance and affirmation. It was another feature of Christ's ministry that He met people whose own sense of inadequacy was confirmed by the whole society around them, and He affirmed their value. My own favourite story is of Zacchaeus – the little man who was a social reject, who had a very low opinion of himself, yet Jesus picked him out and affirmed him:

Entering Jericho he made his way through the city. There was a man there named Zacchaeus; he was superintendent of taxes and very rich. He was eager to see what Jesus looked like; but, being a little man, he could not see for the crowd. So he ran on ahead and climbed a sycamore-tree in order to see him, for he was to pass that way. When Jesus came to the place, he looked up and said, "Zacchaeus, be quick and come down; I must come and stay with you today." He climbed down as fast as he could and welcomed him gladly. At this there was a general murmur of disapproval. "He has gone in", they said, "to be the guest of a sinner." But Zacchaeus stood there and said to the Lord, "Here and now, sir, I give half my possessions to charity; and if I have cheated anyone, I am ready to repay him four times over." Jesus said to him, "Salvation has come to this house today! – for this man too is a son of Abraham, and the Son of Man has come to seek and save what is lost."

Luke 19:1–10

This truly represents the impact of Jesus upon those who have a low, destructive self-image. It reflects the faith that everyone has their own specific value and beauty in God's eyes, and this is the basis of the necessary, proper self-love and self-acceptance which are the essential basis for confidence and reassurance. As in the case of forgiveness, what we receive from God we then can learn to spread to others. So our own self-acceptance, the restoring of our own self-image, should in turn help us to restore the self-image of others, to want to encourage people to believe in themselves as valuable. This is of great importance in the mutual encouragement of marriage. Do we say "thank you", or do we take each other for granted? Do we express romantic feelings so that our partner feels romantic? Do we say how much they mean to us? Do we do the things which support and affirm our partner, or just talk about them?

It is not just an affair which can have a shattering effect. There are plenty of other ways in which midlife can bring trauma to a marriage – a clash of loyalties between partner and parents, a conflict of interest between careers, a complete cutting-out of social life, repeated negative reactions in public, a row over a child, even something as unimportant as a holiday plan or alterations to the home. They are usually symptoms of an inner loneliness which has resulted from poor communication and the ensuing resentment and lack of understanding. These things can build up and become a wall between two people, which in turn will damage the self-image and create polarized feelings. To come back across the division, to reopen the caring and romantic way, requires a great deal of self-awareness and forgiveness and then mutual comfort. But this process is essential, and the only way to ensure that a married couple can be loving into middle age.

The Homosexual

I hope I will be forgiven for mostly using the word "homosexual" for both male homosexuals and lesbians, but it seems a convenient shorthand. As I have already suggested, the changing social attitudes to homosexuality affect many people going through midlife. It is essential for Christians to think out the implications. There have been several reports produced by different Churches beginning this process of reappraisal. What I have to say here is a personal point of view, but has much in common with the findings of those reports.

Many heterosexual people know very little about gay people and often only recognize the effeminate and butch stereotypes. The taboos are still strong, and the idea of homosexual relationships remains offensive to some people. Taboos are important, and can express a proper fear of the unacceptable, but they are not an adequate moral guide in themselves. The Christian Church must become better informed about what gay people think and feel, study the Bible's teaching alongside the new insights, and work out the Christian way.

The damage done to individuals in the Church, or through the influence of the Church, because of their homosexuality, has sometimes been a matter of shame, and has contributed to the despair of many members of the gay community, the suppression of proper affection, and the "escape" into a secret world of tragic promiscuity and non-relationships. The reaction to the AIDS virus has sometimes seemed to suggest that the punishment of God has been properly measured out on these "perverts" – after all, they had the warning of Sodom and Gomorrah! But heterosexual venereal disease, which has been killing people and maiming and handicapping their descendants for generations. The physical risks of infection through hetero- or homosexual promiscuity are great, and can damage totally innocent people. The separation of the sexual act from sustained personal relationships, whether homosexual or heterosexual, is nearly always damaging to the participants and those who relate to them. The key in both cases is to help people find a way to secure, positive relationships, which do not leave them searching in the scrap-heap of human intercourse for some satisfaction and affection.

Even though there remains doubt about some of the causes of a homosexual personality, there is no doubt that a substantial number of people do grow to adulthood attracted to their own sex. Homosexuality is as much part of their personality as heterosexual attraction is for the heterosexual. A young man was subjected by his Christian parents to prolonged nausea therapy to convert him to "normality" – in the process both he, his family and his friends came to see that homosexual *was* "normal" and natural for him. There are people who are born homosexual, there are people who become homosexual, and there are some who have homosexuality thrust upon them. They are homosexuals not by perversion of a heterosexual nature, but because their nature, given and implanted by God through the process of life, has come to be homosexual. Very few homosexuals sustain as far as midlife the idea that by some miracle they could change their orientation, and those who have tried to behave as though they were heterosexual will often give up the attempt.

The teaching of the Bible has obviously been very influential in the formation of the Christian tradition. Homosexual behaviour was commonly accepted in the Mediterranean world in which the Old and New Testaments were written, but the Jewish-Christian community took a firm stand against it, stating that the physical expression of homosexual sexuality was against the will of God.

This general condemnation has been endorsed by the use of the story of Sodom and Gomorrah. This legend has had a far-reaching effect on attitudes and is the source of the word "sodomy", which came to mean sexual intercourse between two men. It is often wrongly believed that the physical expression of male homosexual love necessarily includes anal intercourse. In the story, the cities of Sodom and Gomorrah were destroyed by God with fire and brimstone as a punishment for their wickedness in general, but especially because the men of the city demanded sexual intercourse with Lot's two male guests. Lot was rightly horrified by this demand, but his alternative solution seems to be of highly questionable morality. He says to the men of Sodom:

> Look, I have two daughters, both virgins; let me bring them out to you; . . . but do not touch these men, because they have come under the shelter of my roof.
>
> Genesis 19:8

I think this shows the primitive nature of the story, which cannot provide us with adequate moral guidance. It tells more about the wickedness of abusing people who have come for shelter, about the cruelty and fantasies of men, and the disastrous results of such cruelty, than it does about God and homosexual people.

Leaving this story aside, the Bible on the whole accepts the view that homosexual behaviour is a perversion, practised by heterosexual people. The writers' condemnations were aimed at people who exchanged or gave up their proper heterosexual nature to indulge in perverted homosexual misuse of others. The exploitation of other people of the same sex as a substitute, or an experiment, or to express sexual domination, seems to me to be as wrong now as it was wrong in biblical times. But these texts do not adequately deal with our contemporary understanding. We recognize that a minority of people are homosexual by nature or life experience, and a heterosexual physical relationship would be, in a way, a perversion of their personality. For this reason, it is essential that we find a contemporary Christian morality which takes into account this change, and which can provide the homosexual with a positive ethic for his or her life.

There are many problems and anxieties at the present time for gay people. There are an increasing number of Christian homosexuals who, in their discipleship and prayer, have begun to see a different solution from the tradition of celibacy. They believe that a homosexual relationship can be within the will of God and be the proper destiny and course of their lives. They must have more say about themselves. They are the part of the Body of Christ most concerned about this question and, in a sense, they have to pioneer a new way. It can be morally dubious for heterosexual people to be always laying down the law for gay people, when they don't know the situation from their own experience.

For the homosexual who chooses to be celibate, the problems, difficulties and joys will be similar to those of the celibate heterosexual, although those who belong to single-sex communities will still find themselves living in the heart of their dilemma. But if there is a positive sense of destiny and purpose in the celibate life, reinforced and inspired by the proper rituals of life-vows and living in a praying community, then in some ways that would seem to take the worst sting out of the homosexual condition. There are also many other Christian laity who decide to be celibate. They are often strengthened by the prayers of the people who know them well, and they often receive the reinforcement of God's Spirit and a sense of well-being and worthwhileness, in the midst of their struggle.

Those who recognize that they are homosexual and choose to be celibate, are probably only a minority of Christians who are homosexual, and certainly so of the gay community. It seems to be as impossible and wrong to expect them all to be celibate as it is to expect all heterosexual people to be so. Many already have stable partnerships which are accepted by their friends. Many others live lives of secrecy and private guilt, afraid to admit to anyone – especially to members of the Church – that they are homosexual. Others refuse to admit even to themselves that this is their nature. For all these people, midlife can be a time of increased vulnerability. If they do not come to terms with themselves they can be heading for a bitter, sarcastic and isolated middle age. They may also be pushed by society into a homosexual ghetto and miss out on the heterosexual world in their friendships.

My purpose here is not to tackle the whole question of homosexuality, but to see whether there are any insights which can be gained about the homosexual's journey into middle age.

The homosexual who has never had a physical relationship, because of religious conviction, or fear, or lack of opportunity, can be subject to the same panic in midlife as the heterosexual spinster or bachelor. There can be the desperate feeling that life has passed them by, and they stand on a precipice, wondering whether to jump into the arms of the first person who offers, or risk endless loneliness. In many ways, their pain is greater than that of the heterosexual – if the heterosexual at last finds a partner, everyone will be delighted, but if the virgin homosexual takes the plunge, he may have to face the shock of his own guilt, and possibly the rejection of friends and family. The only alternative might seem to be to withdraw further and further from any relationship where there might be a risk of sexual involvement, and slowly to try to kill off the insistent voice of nature – or sublimate it in some safe, socially acceptable way.

It may be right for such an individual to choose the celibate option with more charity and determination, building the necessary support of other Christians or friends who will give love and encouragement. It may be a help to stop being suspended in the "Shall I? – Shan't I?" anxiety. This decision may also strengthen the sense of identity and free the self from the nagging and persistent sense of guilt. The homosexuality will not, and should not, "go away" because it is an important part of the self, and therefore will have to be expressed through friendships and the love of people who understand. On the other hand, the choice of celibacy could be the wrong way and do nothing to help solve the dilemma, leaving the individual floundering in the same old depression and loneliness. In which case he or she ought to examine, with the help of others, what his or her own attitudes to sexuality really are. If there is no one to talk it through with, then there is the real risk of hopeless adventures. It is more helpful to meet real people who have come to terms with their lives, than to wander around lost and alone in a maze of fantasies. Solutions will not be discovered in solitary confinement.

To tackle the pain of secrecy, it is essential to have friends with whom the whole self-understanding can be shared, and to realize that the taboos applied by parents, relatives and church members create a deep and special need for safe friendships and affection. All Christians know that it is not easy to go on believing that God accepts and loves us "just as I am without one plea", unless there are human beings who also affirm, renew and repeat that love and acceptance of us. It is difficult for forgiveness and healing of the inner self to take place in the love of God, unless there are human beings who also mediate it, express the forgiveness of God and reassure the person that he or she is loved and forgiven. This is not a journey which can be travelled in one day and then be thought of as completed, it is a continuous process, needed right into old age.

If a decision is faced which would change the whole pattern of life, there must be a realistic counting of the cost. Whatever the support received from friends and counsellors, prayer and worship of God are the only solid rocks on which the Christian can find a firm footing in going through this process.

Midlife can also present a real problem for the homosexual couple. They may have lived together for ten or so years in a happy and useful way – enjoying their relationship and the growing social acceptance of their partnership. But they have few of the binding elements to keep them together through their depressed, bored or angry periods. There are no children to care for, and if they split up their possessions can be easily divided. To them, as to heterosexual people, youth seems attractive and beautiful. Society, in spite of growing tolerance, will probably have been hurtful and applied pressure to split them up, and so there will be stored pain and vulnerability, which may lead to the search for the comfort of a new relationship. Although unwanted parenthood is not a threat, the potential damage of infidelity and promiscuity are great.

There are homosexuals who argue that promiscuity is an

inevitable part of the gay life-style. I have not yet heard a convincing argument in support of this assertion, and it seems to be one of the key questions. Promiscuity appears to be an opting out of the cost and value of fidelity, as indeed it does in heterosexual promiscuity. It seems to involve the acceptance of a shallow expression of love and a debasing of the element of trust and commitment. It is not so difficult to understand why homosexuals do not see their relationships as "till death us do part". As I have already said, they have less to bind them than the heterosexual partnerships. But I cannot imagine how infidelity and promiscuity can help sustain a dependable love commitment. Just as in marriage, it is essential for the homosexual partners to keep open the communication between them. How they express their love for each other in private is a matter for themselves alone, according to their own conscience and integrity before God, just as it is in marriage. But their partnership, like any other intimate relationship, will need refreshing, and the "contract" will have to be re-evaluated. In the face of all the difficulties of the gay community, I would like to bear witness to the value and love conveyed by some such partnerships known to me. They are people who will discover what is the right way forward, and the Church and individual Christians should give them every support in their moral journey.

The other main group of homosexuals are those who were pressed, by conformity or lack of self-awareness or religious faith, into marriage. It is often the case that, in spite of a far from satisfactory married sexual relationship, children are conceived and born. Through reading, the media, the experience of friends, these homosexuals realize that their sexual relationship with their wife or husband has been to some extent a pretence, their minimal heterosexual desire wanes and their repressed homosexuality begins to assume enormous importance in their lives. They are then faced with an identity crisis which can be brought to a head at midlife. They begin to feel with increasing urgency that their sexual lives are being totally denied. If they still love their partner, they may be secretly worried about impotence or frigidity. They may experience an all-powerful need for physical expression of their own sexuality, which will be aggravated by the sense that the opportunity will soon be past, because they will lose their attractiveness and potency.

This is a most serious threat to a marriage. There are no easy solutions to such a dilemma. For the bisexual person, the moral choice, to my thinking, is clear. The existing commitment to the family is the paramount moral obligation, and the homosexual side of the bisexual nature should be sublimated. But for the married homosexual who is unable to maintain any sort of physical relationship with their partner, the problem will certainly have to be tackled. Unless the marriage is only a façade, the couple will have to talk it out, and probably will need the advice of a counsellor. Once the truth is out, then they will be freer to decide what their future should be. They may decide to stay together and readjust the relationship. This can work well, but so much depends upon the individuals concerned. Others will decide to separate. For both of them, this process of discovery brings about a fundamental change in their original mutual obligations.

For the homosexual, as for everyone, it is not just a case of working out relationships, but also the continuing attempt to achieve self-understanding. For some people, the cause of their homosexual orientation may be something where healing is still required – "healing" not in the sense of becoming heterosexual, but rather in terms of finding a greater degree of self-acceptance and self-confidence, and being freed from depression. Elizabeth Moberley, in her book *Homosexuality: A New Christian Ethic*, supports the view that the main cause of homosexuality is a deficiency in relationship with the same-sex parent during childhood. She says that because the child felt rejected by the same-sex parent, it mourns for the lost affection, and in adult life

seeks the fulfilment of these "normal" attachment needs.
Moberley, p.9

She suggests that the deficiency can be made up by a sustained, loving, same-sex relationship which is not erotic or physically expressed:

> The needs involved can and should be met independently of sexual activity.
>
> Moberley, p.20

because that is inappropriate to what is fundamentally a parent/child relationship.

A woman I knew spent all her years grieving because her mother abandoned her as a child. In midlife, she found a relationship with a woman just old enough to be her mother. She found great comfort in this. The boundaries between meeting her own mother-need and a lesbian love were narrow. Receiving the mother-comfort only made her more aware of the person she had become through the whole process of her life. The years of loss could not just be reversed, and she knew that she would not find what she wanted until she expressed the love she felt with her whole self.

But some deficiency in relationship with our parents is a universal experience, otherwise we have discovered perfection. Both heterosexual and homosexual people spend a lot of their lives coming to terms with the deficiencies, and benefiting from the strengths, of both or either parent. It is certainly a normal part of the midlife journey to think again how we come to be the person we are, to puzzle out how our parents influenced us and to come to terms with that. There can be a strong element of mourning for a relationship we feel we never had, or which at least was deficient. There is no doubt in my mind that a substitute fatherhood or motherhood can help fill out the parental love we all need but receive in very differing measure. This is certainly not confined to homosexual people, and is only one of the possible causes of their orientation. Deficient relationships with the other-sex parent can also be influential.

I am not, however, under-estimating the importance of parent/child relationships for homosexuals. Because they are mostly single, they often continue to have a more intense relationship with their parents. Any long-term deficiency can therefore go on being a trap, and it will be even more important for the homosexuals to understand their own development and the nature of the relationship. It is possible for mothers or fathers to go on causing the same pain and damage to their children until they die. Somehow it is essential to begin to see why the parent is as he or she is. This may help to develop compassion and understanding for them, and so help the forgiveness process which will free the "child" from bitterness and negative-patterned reactions. Thankfully, there are many homosexual people who find it possible to be open about themselves to their parents, and their parents accept them as they are. When this honesty works, it can lead the way into a far more secure future and loving mutual support.

The Christian homosexual has to try to see his life in the context of the love of God and his own conscience. Self-understanding and self-acceptance based on the love of Christ are the key to the integrity of personality. Because of the disabling effects of people's prejudice, and the apparent conflict with the Christian tradition, it is very important to find allies and people with whom the whole issue can be shared in safety. For those who are uncertain about their identity, or wavering in their midlife, it may help to recognize that part of the need may be personal and not necessarily sexual. It is a time, however, when above all self-awareness is essential, and this should lead to a more decisive approach to life based on that honest self-assessment.

Christian freedom is not a selfish thing, because it involves self-giving love and commitment to the people around us and to the society in which we live. As I shall argue later in this book, our desire for self-realization is limited by the demands of the proper self-realization of the people with whom we are involved. To be self-absorbed leads to isolation and despair. The homosexual condition is in itself not a handicap, though society makes it difficult, nor need it be an immaturity, but rather it is for the homosexual the personality which through birth and life has become their own and is loved by God.

5

Changing Roles

The fast-changing roles of men and women not only profoundly affect our loving into middle age, but also the way families and the wider society operate. Twenty years ago, when I first began interviewing couples who wanted to be married, their expectations of each other were very different from those being expressed now. In 1966, when I asked a man what he wanted of his wife, most basically wanted her to be rather like the delectable perfect wife described in the Book of Proverbs. I can't resist quoting the whole passage:

> Who can find a capable wife?
> Her worth is far beyond coral.
> Her husband's whole trust is in her,
> and her children are not lacking.
> She repays him with good, not evil,
> all her life long.
> She chooses wool and flax
> and toils at her work.
> Like a ship laden with merchandise
> she brings home food from far off.
> She rises while it is still night
> and sets meat before her household.
> After careful thought she buys a field
> and plants a vineyard out of her earnings.
> She sets about her duties with vigour
> and braces herself for the work.
> She sees that her business goes well,
> and never puts out her lamps at night.
> She holds the distaff in her hand,
> and her fingers grasp the spindle.
> She is open-handed to the wretched
> and generous to the poor.

She has no fear for her household when it snows,
for they are wrapped in two cloaks.
She makes her own coverings,
and clothing of fine linen and purple.
Her husband is well known in the city gate
when he takes his seat with the elders of the land.
She weaves linen and sells it,
and supplies merchants with their sashes.
She is clothed in dignity and power
and can afford to laugh at tomorrow.
When she opens her mouth, it is to speak wisely,
and loyalty is the theme of her teaching.
She keeps her eye on the doings of her household
and does not eat the bread of idleness.
Her sons with one accord call her happy;
her husband too, and he sings her praises:
"Many a woman shows how capable she is;
but you excel them all."
Charm is a delusion and beauty fleeting;
it is the God-fearing woman who is honoured.
Extol her for the fruit of all her toil,
and let her labours bring her honour in the city gates.

Proverbs 31:10–31

In spite of the changes, there are still a substantial number of men and children who favour this role for the woman in their life, but are reluctant to admit it. It is sad that women in their battle do not seem to see that this ideal is perfectly justifiable for the woman who, of her own will, chooses it. So often, a woman will say "I'm just a housewife", as though she ought to apologize for caring for a home and the people who live in it. It is a damaging piece of indoctrination that a woman who chooses to be a housewife and mother should somehow feel she is a failure, because she does not have another job. It still remains a great gift to offer to society, and to the family in particular, to provide a secure, loving and hospitable base for the development of the children and for the expression of the extended family. There need be no sense of inferiority in making such a choice. All she must do is to take steps early on to ensure that she has a life and inward centre of her own, because when the children leave, as they will if she has done her job well, a large gap will be left if she tries to fill her life with looking after the home and her husband.

But the key issue here is whether the women have made their own choice to spend their life in that way. Many others choose a different role or combination of roles, either at the start or during the experience of marriage and being a partner. To many women, the total dedication to the home, the husband and the children, can be a rather narrow and even stifling experience. The "I'm just a housewife" syndrome is usually at its strongest when the woman feels that everyone else is doing more interesting and rewarding things than she is, and she realizes just how trapped she feels, being confined to her domestic task. She sees in society around her the possible alternative, where she has a life of her own, where she is not just dependent on her husband and her children for her social relationships, where her mind is more tested and where she can gain satisfaction from doing a job well and from receiving her own income. It will often be in midlife that she is faced with this tension at its most severe, and the way in which she and her partner deal with it will make all the difference between midlife being a crisis or just a creative change in life-style.

Her discovery of her own contribution beyond the home and her family can transform her whole image of herself, make her more interesting, because she is! Her work will bring more material, education and leisure opportunities, not just for her, but for the whole family, and they may begin to enjoy the fruits of her new style. It should not surprise anyone that so many of the facets of life enjoyed by men who have work would be just as enjoyable and stimulating for women. The reverse will also be true, that where there are no jobs, or the jobs available are themselves degrading and monotonous, or even carry too much agonizing responsibility, it will bring similar stress or boredom. But once the freedom and self-reliance have been tasted, there is no going back. The Namibian women in the refugee camps in Angola have learnt a new understanding of the role of women, and now they say, "We shall never be kept in the kitchen again."

Husbands and wives have sometimes tended to assume that this great change in our family structure can be made without affecting the children. Through work with families and projects for latch-key children, I have seen how damaging the empty home can be for children returning from school or in the school holidays. Because of the need for single parents to work, and the fact that often both husband and wife are working, more and more children are deprived of the security which the always-available mother provided. I have no doubt that the lack of a secure home base has been one of the factors responsible for the more rapid brutalization of children who have been left to cope with the streets without the back-up of available parents or other adults. Steps, therefore, have to be taken by the couple or the single parent to make alternative provision. The whole burden of this does not have to fall on the wife. It may well be that the father can be home at the necessary time because of shift work, etc. There may be a grandparent or an elderly neighbour who would enjoy being an adoptive granny – an arrangement that can help all the people involved. There can be play schemes which provide the child with a happy alternative to going home. Whatever provision is made – and I believe it must be – then after this the parents must recognize that they must not be "too tired" to give their children the attention and space they need with them. Both mother and father must create the necessary sense of security in the time they are together. It is time, availability and home which count – not cash. The frightening alienation of some teenagers is caused directly by their never being sure of their parents' love or attention when they were younger. I have known this to arise out of poverty, where a single mother has had to work nights and days to cope with her family's financial needs. But it also happens where there is no need, and where the parents have simply evaded their responsibility. It has to be worked out together, and in the new pattern is a shared task.

It is encouraging that many women who start work actually rediscover their enthusiasm for being a mother, because they do not feel trapped. With adequate back-up, this can be very beneficial – not just for her, but for her children and her husband.

The men's liberation movement does not have the same following or energy as its counterpart. I don't even know whether it exists. Because we are waking up to the stifling attitudes and closed systems which can imprison and restrict women, the war seems to be being waged on that liberation front. But I suppose that, whilst women's liberation is the most prominent battle of the sexes, an underground war is taking place in the men's zone.

Many of us men are confused, but it's not part of the male role to admit it. We will water the garden, clean the car, storm out to the pub, escape into golf, fight back our tears, show we can go it alone, and, above all, busy ourselves in our work.

We know in our hearts that we have to change, but we try to avoid it. At forty we may be faced with the fundamental question, "What's our life for?" – and duck away from it. If we cannot find this ability to change, we shall probably make life miserable for our wife and children, for the people we work with, and mostly for ourselves. It is as though we believe that midlife crises, like religion, are best left to women. We can find ways of side-stepping the question. We will perhaps do anything except the one thing which we ought to do; that is, get through the painful experience of inner change and find the renewed and growing self.

I remember once sitting in a discussion group of priests and crying for half an hour. After the meeting, I crept away and hid myself in my room with the shame of it. Only during the night of doubt and sorrow which followed did it dawn on me that, in weeping, I had done the only sensible and truly male thing to do. The situation called for tears. How often I have thanked God that the Man I follow is reported as having wept when necessary:

Horror and dismay came over him, and he said to them,

"My heart is ready to break with grief; stop here, and stay awake." Then he went forward a little, threw himself on the ground, and prayed that, if it were possible, this hour might pass him by.

Mark 14:33–35

Recently, the Prime Minister of Australia wept in public because he was talking about the suffering of his daughter. The cameras zoomed in, strong men muttered over their pints that such a man should not be Prime Minister, and he fell from power. Maybe the electorate were right to get rid of him, but not if it was just for that reason. Because he is Prime Minister, is he to cease being a father and a man? What sort of monster would that be? Crying is important for us all, and it is often the necessary and sane response to what is happening to us. Yet, from the propaganda of the stiff upper lip as a boy to the essential control at the funeral of our loved ones, the crying is still fairly taboo for us.

Ian Suttee, in a book called *The Origins of Love and Hate*, wrote about the Taboo on Tenderness:

The most typical example . . . can be found in the "gang" of larger and smaller boys who idealize what is called euphemistically "manliness", in contradiction to "babyishness" and "girlishness". The ideals of such a community are intensely anti-feminist, as indicated by the coining of such opprobrious epithets as "milk-sop", "cry-baby", "mummy's boy". On the positive side this ego-ideal holds up "toughness", aggressiveness, hardness, etc., as prime virtues.

Suttee, pp.86–87

Although the "opprobrious epithets" have changed to "wets", "do-gooders", "nigger lovers", "pansies", "wimps", etc., etc., the taboo remains strong. Stand in any pub or football ground, listen to any Board of Directors, sit in a soldiers' mess, and you will hear the taboos reinforced over and over again. Male nurses have had to take more stick from

99

men than from women. One of the main causes of stress amongst the police is their having to face up to violence, tragedy and hatred, yet at the same time being unable to admit weakness, the need of comfort, or a good cry.

The desire for tenderness can be a key factor in the male midlife crisis. This can be seen in some affairs where a man's marriage has become combative, and the anxieties and stress carried by his wife have made her angry and aggressive. He is in the middle of a competitive world where he is expected to be all male and yet, at the same time, he is yearning for tenderness which he finds difficult to express and receive. Fathers often find in their daughters the one place where they can focus their tenderness – she at least will receive and respond without suspicion to his gentle love. A woman once told me (she was the bread-winner in her family) that she used to read the paper when her husband made love to her. Neither she nor anyone else seems to have recognized that when her husband was sent to prison for committing incest, he had had a crisis too. I have seen marriages where the wife wants deep down nothing more than romantic love and tenderness in her husband, which by nature can arouse the desired stronger side of their relationship, and the husband wants tenderness as well. The tragedy is that they have got into a trap so that they cannot express it.

A great deal of damage has been done by the too easy use of the masculine and feminine image. For instance, if feminine means partly intuitive and gentle, then there are certainly many men who have a great deal of both. If masculine means tough and decisive, then there are certainly many women who can demonstrate both qualities. It is part of a normal midlife process for the male and the female to shake off the false stereotypes.

In talking with men, I have found a desire for tenderness and the gentler qualities which they do not feel able to admit anywhere else – not at their work, not in their social life, and, most tragically, not to their wives. There are signs of hope here, as this taboo seems to be breaking a little amongst the young, who can see a desire for peace as manly; who have no difficulty in not only changing their baby's nappy, but enjoying it, and not being ashamed to enjoy it; who have women as friends and colleagues, without needing to see them as candidates for conquest. But the taboo still causes a great deal of inward suffering, and hurts a wider circle of people than just the poor confused man in the middle. If the man can allow his own so-called feminine characteristics out into his own integrated self, he often discovers that it affects his whole way of coping with life. He will need to defeat other people less, he will look for and work for greater co-operation between colleagues, and he will discover the richness of the male-female co-operation in building the just society. If he doesn't resolve it, he may feel it necessary all the time to show how hard he is, and so need to reduce the contribution that others might make.

"But," says the Managing Director, "if I allow my own feelings to emerge, or am sensitive to the needs of the families of our workforce, how shall I ever make the decision to make them redundant?" The "real" world is tough as nails, and marshmallow sensitivity and sentimentality only lead to disaster. I have some sympathy with that argument in this viciously competitive society. But I would argue that greater sensitivity may lead to better man-management, that many companies who make people redundant do have the necessary resources to put into their reorientation process and resettlement, that an understanding of poverty and environmental damage would strengthen, not weaken, the conduct of business.

There is no doubt that the nature of the man's midlife crisis will be strongly influenced by the sort of work he does. The clergyman, the doctor, the probation officer and any others who have spent their lives so far attempting to care for others, by being totally at their disposal – "availability" is the great thing – may suddenly find in their midlife that their own self rebels and asks, "What about me? Isn't it time I had some space and found out who I am and what creative gifts I possess?" I once had a terrifying nightmare, which in the telling sounds patronizing and self-righteous – but then I probably was. I dreamt I was a large white fish, floating dead in a pond. There were hundreds of little fish tearing at the flesh until there was nothing left. As I share with my colleagues in evaluating their work, one of the most important questions is, "And what about you?" The caring role can lead to self-annihilation, and it can have happened for years before anyone notices. A doctor friend of mine had a breakdown, and in the end its cause was found to be the unresolved grief the doctor had experienced which had never been allowed expression because of the paramount responsibility to care for others. Sometimes the insistence on proper self-love, which we dole out to others, we are incapable of applying to ourselves.

On the other hand, the man whose task has been industrial, or fiercely competitive, may well look for some more personal or spiritual role as he approaches middle age. Training engineers and accountants for the priesthood used to be an exhilarating process, as their lives expanded and they found greater fulfilment in the new spiritual journey and the expression of love and care. There are many city gents who become very much involved in voluntary organizations and apply their spare energy to charity, as they experience the restrictions of their business world. There may well be a desire for exploring the person inside them who has been bottled up in his role.

Men do considerable violence to themselves by refusing to allow their gentler side to emerge. Pretending to be what we are not, refusing to admit our feelings, even to ourselves, disables us. It can lead to the loss of our own real self, behind the role we believe the male should play. Of course, staying vulnerable is more costly – but not in the long run, because the sustained hypocrisy and pretence lead to a disfigured personality.

Just as the man may be needing tenderness, so a woman might at the same time be going in the opposite direction. Jung said of marriage:

It is not hard to imagine what will happen when the

husband discovers his tender feelings and the wife her sharpness of mind.

Quoted in Sheehy, p.171

It is unlikely that men and women will go through their midlife crisis at the same calendar age, or at the same time, and it is quite likely that they will seem to be moving in opposite directions.

A man in midlife may well feel like saying to his wife, "Why do you want to get a job?" He may well be heartily sick of his work, and be genuinely puzzled why she wants to get into all that burden. Hearing all those mums who say "I'm just a housewife", and seeing the new light in a woman's eye when she has a job after years of child-rearing, the question "Why?" seems worth some study.

Money is obviously important – not so much to get it in the bank, but because of the feeling of freedom and independence it can bring. If only people who suggest voluntary solutions for unemployment would realize how much money means to the sense of identity in an affluent, secular society. But when a woman starts work in midlife, this new wage is "her" money, and she has the right to decide priorities and how it is spent. It is also important because it gives some resources to enable the woman to live to her own best image of her self – both in appearance and in self-reliance. Money may be desperately necessary – either at the poverty level or at other levels in how the needs of the woman and her family are perceived. If it has always been a struggle to buy clothes for the children, to pay for school trips, to have a holiday, to replace broken household equipment, then the extra income brings relief from this anxiety, and therefore a greater freedom. In reality, once we are above survival level, money often frees us from the burden of one set of living standards, only to introduce and titillate us into desiring a higher set filled with even more experiences which in turn create a demand for even more money.

But, though money is important, I do not believe it anywhere near explains the new light in the eye, sense of purpose in the step, and growth of self-confidence which frequently develop when a woman is able to take up her career again, or perhaps start doing a job for the first time. It is a demonstration of the importance for our self-esteem of our understanding of our role in life.

The propaganda begins to work early when people are facing their last years at school, and teachers and parents, uncles and aunts, friends and neighbours ask what they are going to do when they leave school. It is almost a compulsive question. As a Bishop, meeting hundreds of children, I can't quite give it up. It would be totally amazing if a boy said, "I would like to be married, to look after our children and create a nice home." Interestingly enough, no girl has ever given me that answer either. Yet both girls and boys probably think that having a family will be a major part of their lives. So we tend to see what we are going to "do" as a job as the justification of our plans for our own future. The raising of a family will just take place along the way. Then the girls, like the boys, will probably do some training and start a job. They receive their pay packet, they have the socializing of work, they have their own agenda which makes legitimate claims on their home timetable, they feel a person in a new way. Add to this, in many teenagers, the frantic desire to leave school and get away from what they regard as the unnecessary restrictions on their adult independence, and it is not difficult to see why getting a job is so important to both the young man and the young woman. If the work they take on involves the building of a career with clearly defined stages of promotion and status, then they both have their ambitions. For the woman there will often be the disadvantage that employers have a nasty suspicion that at any moment she's going to have a baby and disappear for a key period – just when they needed her. There can't be many bosses (male or female) who have not attended the wedding of their brilliant young secretary with mixed feelings that they'll soon be in the dreadful hassle of replacing her. Attitudes are changing, and, through a combination of enlightenment and positive anti-discrimination practice, this "natural break" in a woman's career is becoming more acceptable. My point, however, is this: the society in which we grow up is one which creates the strong expectation that to play our full role in society we ought to do a job. This pressure is continuous, and will often live with a mum as she sees her children grow from the cot to primary school.

We are living in a time when jobs are in short supply, and it looks unlikely that we shall ever return to the stage when anyone who wants a job can get one. It therefore is extremely important to look at "the job" and understand what it brings. As I have already said, the money motive must not be under-estimated. Money brings personal power and freedom from poverty, and opens up the bewildering variety of experience which the world has to offer its richer inhabitants. "The job" also brings recognition. In a time of heavy unemployment, any job at all brings some recognition, even if it is only the dignity of being free from having no work. In times of full employment, or for those who are comfortably off, the nature of the job – whether it is interesting and worthwhile – seems to enter far more highly into our expectations. The arguments we had in the 1960s about boring, tedious, monotonous, anti-social, dehumanizing work seem to have faded out, and now to have any job seems to be much more the be-all and end-all, if it brings in more than the social security equivalent. But, of course, those jobs we argued about in the sixties are still boring, tedious, monotonous, dehumanizing, etc., and yet they have taken on a new dignity because they carry the resource and recognition of *being* work. As technology makes further inroads into the nature of work, machines will increasingly do the repetitive tasks, with less and less human supervision. Meanwhile, society seems to be saying that we shall be able to afford to pay less for the caring and service jobs, which often provide the most rewarding employment for the people who do them. I am not an economist, as will be clear – and I cannot prophesy how we shall solve this dilemma. I only want to make the point that unemployment becomes part of the midlife crisis when a "job" stands for personal identity.

Somehow we shall have to find ways of deriving identity from being usefully and creatively occupied – so that not having a job will not carry the same stigma. For this to happen, there has to be a fair sharing of the available resources.

Midlife appears to be a time when both men and women look for recognition in their own right. They will either be approaching the end of the family-rearing cycle, or they will feel they ought to have established themselves in their careers. The married woman will see it as the time for the expansion of her own horizons, and this will often involve her husband and family in sometimes painful renegotiations of their home life – yet with rewards (not just financial) all round if it can be achieved in a harmonious and mutually supportive way.

The evidence of the passion with which women (I believe rightly) embrace their regained independence, recognition and sense of worth is proof of how important this recognition is for men and women. The sense of identity, of being a real person, of being recognized in our own right, is one of the strong desires we have at all times, but it can reach another crisis point in midlife. Their role in their community and in the employed society does a great deal to foster the sense of worth. The unemployed man who spends hours watching television whilst others are employed, experiences a total loss of role and so suffers a desperate indignity in a society which puts such a high premium on work. The mother who has been confined to the narrow channel of social contact which her husband allows, who does not feel that the mothering of children, the creation of a home and the loving of her husband are her total and final role in life, may well experience the pain of being reduced to nothing. She will probably feel trapped and cabbage-like if she has retained her expectation of doing a "job". This is where we are, and it's no use the man secretly harking back to the good old days when a wife knew her place and played wife and mother to him as required. It is also no use his indulging in the hypocrisy that he wants her to find her expanded independence, but at no cost to himself.

It is sometimes not only husbands, the family and society who prevent the woman from stepping out and taking a more active role outside the family. Gail Sheehy suggests that the main task of a woman in midlife is "to transcend dependency through self-declaration" (p.426). She describes the exhilarating journey which many women make at this stage:

> It is not through more caregiving that a woman looks for a replenishment of purpose in the second half of her life. It is through cultivating talents left half-finished, permitting ambitions once piggybanked, becoming aggressive in the service of her own convictions rather than a passive-aggressive party to someone else's.

Sheehy, p.426

It may be that a woman will find her "self-declaration" in developing her "caregiving". She may be able to use the experience of bringing up her family in supporting others in that task. She may herself have started a career in a caring profession, to which she can return with the great added advantage of her experience as a mother. But it may be that her other gifts and skills are the ones which can be developed.

Yet any attempt to free oneself from dependency is a painful process of new birth. There is such a temptation to cling to the familiar, however restricting it might seem. The role of housewife and mother may seem a whole lot safer than launching out into the deep without a rubber ring! Kierkegaard said that faith was like swimming in the ocean over seventy thousand fathoms. The launching process is risky. Maybe she feels that she has forgotten all she ever learnt, or fears that it's all out of date. "The family would never cope without me" – "He says he wants me to 'go out', but he doesn't really want me to, and he'll make no real changes which would make it possible." It may even be that the woman has tried and it has been a disaster, or she has retreated because she can't cope with the anger which her husband and children are expressing. Or it may be she's sort of grown used to being misused. It is the dress she's comfortable in, or she knows it's uncomfortable, but she's certainly not going to let them do the decent thing and buy her a new one. There can be a rather defeated spirit, and lack of self-confidence, in that the woman colludes with her husband's infantile demands as well as her children's. This is where she needs a bit of old-fashioned grit. Although sometimes I have resented the demands made on my wife by her "self-transcendence", I am thankful that she had the identity and proper self-love to create her opportunity to get back into the "action". If the woman positively chooses to build her midlife spiritual journey through the home and domestic and voluntary responsibilities, that's fine, but if she is trapped into it by her own self-deprecation, lack of self-confidence and masochism, it is a disaster for her and her husband. It is understandable, because, as in so many experiences of life, when you have been misused for long enough, it is difficult to see the freedom staring you in the face and to risk embracing it.

Although I think this change is full of difficulties, I believe that when we have come to terms with it, as some people claim they already have done, then we shall benefit enormously. It is my belief that there is a fullness of life for human beings if there is justice. The psalmist portrays a very positive idea of the human destiny. We are to be co-agents with God in making the world make itself. We are to live as disciples who expect to share in the bringing of God's kingdom. We are to have a vision of the proper management of the earth and the creation of a just society.

When I look up at thy heavens, the work of thy fingers,
the moon and stars set in their place by thee,
what is man that thou shouldst remember him,
mortal man that thou shouldst care for him?
Yet thou hast made him little less than a god,
crowning him with glory and honour.
Thou makest him master over all thy creatures;
thou hast put everything under his feet:
all sheep and oxen, all the wild beasts,

the birds in the air and the fish in the sea,
and all that moves along the paths of ocean.
O Lord our sovereign,
how glorious is thy name in all the earth!

Psalm 8:3–9

This suggests to me that creative employment is a central part of the human life – I use the word "employment", not the word "job". In the Bible the role of the wife in this scheme of God's agency was to be wife and mother and home-builder. That pattern has now been broken, as indeed we should expect patterns to be broken if God goes on creating the earth and His Spirit continues to innovate.

Here and now I will do a new thing; this moment it will break from the bud. Can you not perceive it?

Isaiah 43:19

If our society has been the product of male power and domination, then I can only hope that we can recognize that these changing roles are a movement of God's Spirit, to be welcomed with joy and its accompanying pain.

6

Revising Ambition

The changing roles of men and women also affect the exercise of power and authority in our society. The hierarchy of the Church is one of the best examples of how deprived an authority structure can be which remains totally male dominated. Issues of power, authority and impotence, success and failure, concern us at every period of our lives, but often take a critical form as we experience midlife.

For some people, midlife brings success in their field of work with greatly increased responsibility and new, wider horizons. For others, it brings the sad realization that ambitions are not going to be fulfilled, and that their earlier dreams were merely fantasies. The fine points on salary scales and the carefully defined promotion ladders only serve to accentuate how we are doing in this race. Our exact status seems to indicate our progress and our possible future. I have been surprised by the anxiety about status in the Church. We don't seem to be very different from the rest of society. Perhaps it is easy for me to say, as I was made a Bishop in mid-midlife. But there is something serious going on inside the people who are so concerned about an extra title, or degree, or scale post, people who desire their own carefully specified area of responsibility and the accompanying sign of success. The child whose painting is displayed on the school wall has something to show his parents on visiting day. The teenager who is able to put on his application form that he has CSEs, "O" levels and "A" levels, is part of the system which leads to the desire to fill up a curriculum vitae with useful and successful achievements. They don't usually leave spaces for failures, which have to be guessed at by the people making the appointment, by reading between the lines in references as to whether the experiences have been the building bricks of a successful career, or the rubble left after a series of failures.

We are all different, and some of us seem to be driven on by ambition or desire for responsibility, or rewards, whereas others are much more content to be led or to accept a lower status with which we feel comfortable. This mixture of motivation is probably essential to the operation of society, and not in itself a cause for anxiety. If equality of opportunity is offered, it will become abundantly clear that it does not lead to equality of achievement. The danger is much more to be found in how individuals deal with success or mediocrity or failure, if they see their lives in those terms.

The spiritual dangers of success, and the power which goes with it, are great and, in the long run, a far more serious threat to the soul. In accountancy, in the army, and in the Church, I have seen far too much of the personal degeneration which can accompany success to embrace it whole-heartedly as an uncomplicated friend. It is always a remarkable and memorable experience to meet the successful, powerful person who has somehow retained or learnt the humility which is the proper expression of all God's children here on earth. The necessity to win battles, the control over other people's lives, the seductive applause, the arrogance of life-style, the external protection against the small indignities, the growing conviction that we are right, and the necessity to subdue opposition – all these things can lead to a loss of inwardness, and a creation of distance between the successful person and others. Processions, rituals, childish hierarchical squabbles and the more heavily armed struggle of boardroom or staff politics, develop an armour which is both a display of strength and force, and at the same time is covering up the slightest hint of weakness or failure. City dinners, committees, politics, power games, reveal the seduction of what is called, by those who are tiring of it, the rat race. The success, the power, can all become a sort of complicated, but all-consuming projection of the self – the huge picture we have on the wall of the adult world, for everyone to see and admire and recognize. Slowly, without noticing, that external expression of the self becomes so important that the soul is given in its service, along with the wishes, rights and values of other people involved. For instance, ambition can become so all-important that a wife might die off almost without the husband noticing, until she takes to drink, or leaves, or becomes a non-person. Yet the impulsion to succeed will seem such a profoundly good reason, whatever the sacrifices which have to be made on its altar.

This aggressive approach to life can then begin to eliminate the child in us. This in turn makes us more domineering and controlling. We lose the ability to embrace failure, to hear and receive the truth. The power becomes addictive, even though the responsibility it brings looks like a killer, and sometimes is. The power usually brings higher material expectations at a time when leisure, comfort, food and drink become even more attractive, and this in turn can blind us to the poor and hungry of our world. Midlife can be a time when the decisive battles are fought, which either bring the desired success or which lead to disappointment and frustration because progress is so slow or is not there at all.

For the Christian, success can be a trap, and Jesus seems to have majored on it. On the question of power, He has this to say:

> You know that in the world, rulers lord it over their subjects, and their great men make them feel the weight of authority; but it shall not be so with you. Among you, whoever wants to be great must be your servant, and whoever wants to be first must be the willing slave of all — like the Son of Man; he did not come to be served, but to serve, and to give up his life as a ransom for many.
>
> Matthew 20:25–28

Even if it is something such as wisdom or knowledge or skill which we pursue, it all looks frail, transient and paltry before the wisdom, love and knowledge of God. The epistle of James has some practical advice:

> Who among you is wise or clever? Let his right conduct

give practical proof of it, with the modesty that comes of wisdom. But if you are harbouring bitter jealousy and selfish ambition in your hearts, consider whether your claims are not false, and a defiance of the truth. This is not the wisdom that comes from above; it is earth-bound, sensual, demonic. For with jealousy and ambition come disorder and evil of every kind. But the wisdom from above is in the first place pure; and then peace-loving, considerate, and open to reason; it is straightforward and sincere, rich in mercy and in the kind deeds that are its fruit.

James 3:13–17

And as for a sense of self-importance:

My brothers, believing as you do in our Lord Jesus Christ, who reigns in glory, you must never show snobbery. For instance, two visitors may enter your place of worship, one a well-dressed man with gold rings, and the other a poor man in shabby clothes. Suppose you pay special attention to the well-dressed man and say to him, "Please take this seat", while to the poor man you say, "You can stand; or you may sit here on the floor by my footstool", do you not see that you are inconsistent and judge by false standards?

Listen, my friends. Has not God chosen those who are poor in the eyes of the world to be rich in faith and to inherit the kingdom he has promised to those who love him?

James 2:1–5

The basis of this requirement of holiness – that power is to be exercised with humility and in service – derives from the belief that we have seen God in Jesus.

Let your bearing towards one another derive out of your life in Christ Jesus. For the divine nature was his from the first; yet he did not think to snatch at equality with God, but made himself nothing, assuming the nature of a slave.

113

Bearing the human likeness, revealed in human shape, he humbled himself, and in obedience accepted even death – death on a cross.

> Philippians 2:5–8

And the implication is that power and success are a risky business for the disciple of Jesus:

So you too, my friends, must be obedient . . . You must work out your own salvation in fear and trembling; for it is God who works in you, inspiring both the will and the deed, for his chosen purpose.

> Philippians 2:12–13

The terrifying thing about Dives, the rich man, was not only that he did nothing for Lazarus, the beggar at his gate, but that he did not *see* reality because of his own self-importance. Midlife for the potentially successful and powerful is a time when they may set out on the road to self-righteousness and arrogance, or when they begin to see that life needs an inner purpose, and that all the splendour of success is transitory. In Canterbury Cathedral, Archbishop Henry Chichele had his tomb built while he was still alive. On top of the tomb is his effigy, robed in the splendour of cope and mitre, but underneath is the skeleton he would become. It was a reminder, to him and to everyone, of his mortality, and a warning against thinking of himself more highly than he ought to think. The Christian who has worldly power and authority will need to develop a strong sense of inwardness, and pray that he will understand how it is between him and God. It is essential that Christian people do not shy away from worldly or ecclesiastical responsibility and authority, in an attempt to keep themselves pure and unsullied by this naughty world, but rather should recognize increasingly their dependence on God and the priority of the loving service of others in following the One who washed His disciples' feet. "Salutations in the market place", the weight of authority, robes of distinction, media attention, are not what puts us right with God. Worldly success can never be the Christian justification. Before God, we are minor technicians, apprentices and novices all our lives.

> If there is anyone among you who fancies himself wise – wise I mean by the standards of this passing age – he must become a fool to gain true wisdom. For the wisdom of the world is folly in God's sight.
>
> 1 Corinthians 3:18–19

There is this sense of everything being turned upside down because we think as man thinks and not as God thinks. Jesus was clear that it was not possible to serve God and Mammon, which could be translated as money or worldly success. In His own temptations, Jesus was rejecting both power (the ruler over all the kingdoms) and material success (living by bread alone). For those, therefore, who are by midlife set upon the path to success, there should be fear and trembling, lest their soul should be forfeit.

> Then he said to the people, "Beware! Be on your guard against greed of every kind, for even when a man has more than enough, his wealth does not give him life." And he told them this parable: "There was a rich man whose land yielded heavy crops. He debated with himself: 'What am I to do? I have not the space to store my produce. This is what I will do,' said he: 'I will pull down my storehouses and build them bigger. I will collect in them all my corn and other goods, and then say to myself, "Man, you have plenty of good things laid by, enough for many years: take life easy, eat, drink, and enjoy yourself." ' But God said to him, 'You fool, this very night you must surrender your life; you have made your money – who will get it now?' That is how it is with the man who amasses wealth for himself and remains a pauper in the sight of God."
>
> Luke 12:15–21

The highly successful and powerful, however, are a minority

group. Most of us have to face up to mediocrity in midlife. We begin to see our life's setting and the boundaries of our ambition. Some will accept those limitations happily whilst others agonize, become frustrated and get damaged and even swallowed up by resentment. We may use up a great deal of energy because we were passed over, because someone else was promoted before us, because no one else can see as clearly as we can what our qualifications deserve. There are a great many disappointed people about. Such an attitude can begin to build a negative middle age and an embittered old age. It may be true that the "powers that be" have been unjust, that we've had bad luck, and we eat our heart out saying "If only this" and "If only that", but envy is a crippling experience, and it makes the envious a victim twice. We are a victim because we do not have what we believe we deserve, and we are a victim because we live with the bitterness entailed in the envy itself. It brings the misery of the lower nature, and reflects the opposition of that nature to God. Like most sins, it is very understandable. There cannot be many people who have not experienced it – the whole range of human envy, from the first moment they thought their mum or dad loved their brother/sister more than them, to the Cabinet Minister who believed he should have been Foreign Secretary or even Prime Minister. It appears in the Bible as the root of the second great fall of mankind, leading to the first murder, Cain's envy of his brother Abel:

> The day came when Cain brought some of the produce of the soil as a gift to the Lord; and Abel brought some of the first-born of his flock, the fat portions of them. The Lord received Abel and his gift with favour; but Cain and his gift he did not receive. Cain was very angry and his face fell.
>
> Genesis 4:3–5

If we think more highly of ourselves than we ought to think, then the pain of envy can be the route by which we come to a more accurate and realistic view of our own ability. If there is

116

a real injustice in our situation, such as not being given a job because we are black, or because we have stuck to a principle, then in a sense we are identified with the struggle to bring about God's kingdom. Our battle is part of the battle to create a just society. But for us as individuals, caught in a midlife trap where our careers have got stuck and our great expectations have had their wings clipped, there is a spiritual problem. It may be that, discovering we are up a cul-de-sac, we shall go back to the main road and set off in a totally different direction. This may be the right thing to do, and may indeed be what God is wanting us to do. Many people engage creatively in a second career or new life-style, and find fulfilment – not least those who become priests.

But such a sharp change may not be possible, nor even desirable, and the proper course will be to accept the reduced aspiration and surrender the more exalted future. There may be great riches in the job we are already doing, or a job like it. The parish priest who thought he ought to be a Dean, in prayer will perhaps slowly rediscover the holiness and the awesome responsibility of being a good parish priest. The teacher who believes he should have been Head may recognize that the children – each one of them – are the most vulnerable and precious responsibility, and that it doesn't really matter whether there are forty or fifteen hundred to care for. A more realistic view of the headmaster's job would show that he has even less time for children, and that administration can so easily become the centre of his own role in life.

Whether we are in industry or commerce or in the caring professions, there are nearly always opportunities to contribute not just to the work, but to the work people. I know a roadsweeper who does his job extremely well, but who also is to be seen most days talking to someone and humanizing his horrible road. We know a local hairdresser who provides a community group, mutual advice centre and therapy session with tea and buns – under the guise of doing people's hair. I've known many people who have accepted their career disappointments and found a whole range of other ways of expressing their fulfilment – through voluntary interests and by love of people. The pursuit of a career can be a totally absorbing drive which may result in personal failures in the higher gifts of love and faith. Busyness can prevent people from seeing the person behind the eyes, having time for other people, being able to offer simple, spontaneous help and service. There are people who accept the middle road, the more "mediocre" position, and then find they have the space and the energy in the rest of their lives to take responsibilities in the local community, in the Church, or in the necessary struggle for justice in our world. There is plenty of space and opportunity for fulfilment if we learn to accept inside ourselves what seems to be God's will for us. As I shall try to say in my last chapter, our lives ought to be far more about "being" than they are.

> Think of the ravens: they neither sow nor reap; they have no storehouses or barns; yet God feeds them.
>
> Luke 12:24

And just in case we have not got the message:

> While they were on their way, Jesus came to a village where a woman named Martha made him welcome in her home. She had a sister, Mary, who seated herself at the Lord's feet and stayed there listening to his words. Now Martha was distracted by her many tasks, so she came to him and said, "Lord, do you not care that my sister has left me to get on with the work by myself? Tell her to come and lend a hand." But the Lord answered, "Martha, Martha, you are fretting and fussing about so many things; but one thing is necessary. The part that Mary has chosen is best; and it shall not be taken away from her."
>
> Luke 10:38–42

God will not allow us to justify ourselves through success or activism; our justification is through God in us. When I have done sixteen hours' work for six days a week, I know that my dear friend, who has no job, but visits an old neighbour three times a day and brings her peace of mind, is just as near, if not nearer, to the eternal life for which I – like many others, perhaps all of us – am searching.

In terms of life's ambitions, "contentment" always seems popular! It looks like a good aim for the midlife. The only sentence of Horace I remember from schooldays' Latin is *Quid non contentus homo sit?*, which, being approximately interpreted, means "Why is man never contented with his lot?"

Certainly contented people can seem pretty relaxing to be with, and appear to create the least amount of disruption. There is something beautiful about "contentment" against the odds. The person struggling against disability or illness who finds the peace of mind to be content is an inspiration, as is the person who is content because she lives for others and provides stability in a shaky and disturbed society. There are some individuals within an extended family or an institution who provide a steadiness by not winding themselves up too high, and maintaining consistent and reliable ballast in the storm. There are people who are spiritually content. By nature, their relationship with God is like an unruffled lake and they reflect His peace. But there is a contentment too which is claustrophobic, and may be in league with the destructive trends in our society. The well-fed rabbits in *Watership Down* appeared at first sight to the struggling Hazel and his hard-pressed followers to be extremely content and well-off. But that paradise of good grazing and secure environment was built upon a massive self-deception. They had lulled themselves into a false sense of security, and refused to face up to the reality that their numbers were regularly culled. It was not long before Hazel and Co. decided they would prefer to be "out there" where all the dangers were. There can be a narrow line between contentment and self-satisfaction and stagnation. A pond becomes stagnant because there is no current and it is not refreshed by the stream. Somehow I think that contentment is the proper goal of the last chapter of our lives, and that people who fall into it too early can solidify their own well-being and ignore or turn their backs on the suffering around them.

Security, comfort and contentment can settle into a selfish spirit, so that what might be a reservoir becomes silted and does not provide water for the city. To the self-satisfied, the Bible has some disturbing words to say. God is so often used to baptize and conserve the vested interests of the contented. But God is not mocked. He calls us to faith and trust as we follow our own pilgrimage. We should not expect to be too much at home in this life. The journey with God is often disturbing, and calls for heroism. Hazel's small, hard-pressed group of rabbits was a pilgrim band – they shared in the mystery of freedom. There can be no contentment in the deep sense until God's kingdom comes and there is no hunger, no poverty, no greed. We are a long way from that kingdom, and our so-called stability is preserved by our willingness to possess a massive armoury and hold the power to destroy the world and contaminate the universe. Our stability is also based on others' poverty and, in the long run, will not prove to be stability at all. It is not time for contentment.

If our own lot is in a fair ground, then we should look outwards to build the possibility for others. The relationship we have with God's Spirit will challenge us to expand our mind and spirit and our generosity of life. To retire from the pilgrimage in midlife is to close down the potential for our own being. Comfortable Britain or Comfortable Wherever-it-might-be, creates a comfortable God in its own image and likeness – it will be no time before God's will is more easily identified with comfortable objectives. The "Comforter" – the name of the Holy Spirit – is the One who brings comfort to those who engage in their pilgrimage. He stands alongside them in their struggle as an advocate, He does not deal out palliatives or say "peace" where there is no peace. Uncomfortable Revelation can sting the sleeping:

To the angel of the church at Laodicea write:

"These are the words of the Amen, the faithful and true witness, the prime source of all God's creation: I know all your ways; you are neither hot nor cold. How I wish you were either hot or cold! But because you are lukewarm, neither hot nor cold, I will spit you out of my mouth. You say, 'How rich I am! And how well I have done! I have everything I want.' In fact, though you do not know it, you are the most pitiful wretch, poor, blind, and naked."

Revelation 3:14–17

I am not used to working amongst powerful or notably successful people in the world's terms. There seem to be more who consider themselves to be failures than successes, and who struggle to find what contentment they can in difficult circumstances. It may be that my East London ministry has affected my survey! I meet so many people who experience a crushing sense of failure or an overwhelming sense of inadequacy, or too many pressures to be coped with. Sometimes they appear brash, self-confident and aggressive, but that is often a deception. Inside they don't feel they have much to offer. Jesus told a parable:

It was aimed at those who were sure of their own goodness and looked down on everyone else. "Two men went up to the temple to pray, one a Pharisee and the other a tax-gatherer. The Pharisee stood up and prayed thus: 'I thank thee, O God, that I am not like the rest of men, greedy, dishonest, adulterous; or, for that matter, like this tax-gatherer. I fast twice a week; I pay tithes on all that I get.' But the other kept his distance and would not even raise his eyes to heaven, but beat upon his breast, saying, 'O God, have mercy on me, sinner that I am.' It was this man, I tell you, and not the other, who went home acquitted of his sins. For everyone who exalts himself will be humbled; and whoever humbles himself will be exalted."

Luke 18:9–14

I would say that the parable was also aimed to encourage

121

those who thought very little of themselves. The two men symbolize for me the attitudes of most people not only to God, but to life. It is one of the fundamental divisions, this self-righteousness and the humble realism. Jesus, on several occasions, inferred that the truly holy person was often the last person to realize their own goodness. It was a secret even from the righteous themselves that they were close to God.

> Then the righteous will reply, "Lord, when was it that we saw you hungry and fed you, or thirsty and gave you drink, a stranger and took you home, or naked and clothed you? When did we see you in prison, and come to visit you?" And the king will answer, "I tell you this: anything you did for one of my brothers here, however humble, you did for me."
>
> Matthew 25:37–40

Just as Jesus had a warning for the successful, the rich, the powerful and the self-righteous, so also He had a word of love, encouragement and assurance for those who could see no value in themselves or in their lives.

To me, it has always been a wonder of the Christian faith which I have not found anywhere else, and which stemmed from the lived-out life of the Man Jesus, that He saw a value in people that neither they themselves nor others appreciated. In one sense, the heroic people in the gospels are often broken, vulnerable people with a low self-image.

> Sir, who am I to have you under my roof? You need only say the word and the boy will be cured.
>
> Matthew 8:8

This cannot be a mock humility which is switched on when we go to church. As Kierkegaard said, that would be like laughing at a joke because someone told you it was funny. This humility is rather something inside a person who has dethroned the self and comes to God and to life recognizing the stains and the failures. This uncomfortable demand of the Gospel remains one of the main reasons why people reject the reality of God. It is, of course, perfectly possible, as Jesus' parables showed, to accept the reality of God as a theory, and yet to remain secure in our own self-righteousness.

There are those, however, who become addicted to failure or who "nurse" their suffering lest it should get better. This is not just self-pity – that well-defined road which leads to nowhere – it is deeper than that. I first recognized this in myself. If things were going badly for me, and I had a real cause for feeling sorry for myself, I would for a mysterious reason take steps to make it worse. It is a sort of "self-destruct" button. Ever since I caught myself doing it – trying to head the league table of the badly-done-by – I have naturally been able to spot many other people doing it. It is some sort of self-punishment which, in its severest form, can reduce the self to nothing. It is partly a way of saying to the world, "Wake up and realize how miserable I am", and partly a way of expressing the resentment we feel against the world and ourselves for letting us get into that position. It is also partly a reaction to the despair of feeling that nothing can be done, or that no one truly wants to help. When people are unemployed they feel deeply hurt, and they will often refuse to accept the opportunities of occupying themselves which are offered to them. There is so much they could do in their community, but they cannot.

I have known wives who feel they are being misused by their husbands and their children, and yet even when offers of help are given, they cannot accept them. Somehow that would let the family off the hook, and the wife would lose the one hold she has over them. This is a familiar reaction, and easily understood by anyone who has tasted the depression caused by feeling nothing or less than nothing, a doormat on which everyone wipes their feet as they dash in and out. This addiction to failure and inadequacy can be very difficult to shift, and people can get into a pattern of reactions which they wouldn't know how to escape if the opportunity was presented. It is a little like the bird trapped in a room, who keeps on beating its head against the windows when the door has been opened to let it out. It carries with it the added pain that it leaves no room for others to change, because whatever steps they take, there is no trust that they mean it or will sustain it. In such a case, a midlife crisis may well be essential in the hope of preventing a perpetual path of misery by bringing things to a head. This is where hope is so important. Unfortunately hope cannot be injected. Other people, by their love and changing, can prepare a way for hope, but it is a virtue which has to grow inside ourselves.

It is my belief that hope is a beautiful gift of God, and it can be found and unwrapped in prayer. It is sad, however, to see the number of people who say they are too miserable, too unhappy, to pray. Sometimes people will stay away from church for months, and then say that they have felt too miserable to come. It is almost as though they are determined not to let God off the hook either. People say, "I'm not good enough to go to church." When you think of the nature of Jesus, His teaching and His promise, you can appreciate why the opposite should be true – "I'm not good enough *not* to go." But prayer doesn't just happen in church, and it is important to remember that it is the God of hope as well as of love to whom we pray. There seems to be an internal personal mystery which takes a person out of self-pity and self-hurt into hope and a rebuilding of the sense of identity. Sometimes the crisis is necessary to make other people take the cries for help seriously – it is amazing how insensitive we can all be to the pain and misery of those nearest to us.

In a chronic state of depression, it is not enough just to find the trigger which set it off, because there will have been so many triggers which are confused behind the veil of our own self-understanding. Jesus told another parable which has a cutting edge for those who have ears to hear it. It concerns a man who was going abroad and wanted his capital to be managed by his agents:

> . . . to one he gave five bags of gold, to another two, to another one, each according to his capacity.
>
> Matthew 25:15

The first two took some risks, and doubled their money, but the third, who only had one bag to begin with, was afraid of losing even that:

> Master, I knew you were a hard man; you reap where you have not sown, you gather where you have not scattered; so I was afraid and I went and hid your gold under the ground.
>
> Matthew 25:24–25

The master, like all good capitalists, was not at all pleased that he had not doubled his money, and he made the poor man severely redundant. This story is not really about gold, nor is it about entrepreneurial flair; it is about what we believe about ourselves, our value, and then how boldly we give ourselves to life. The reason why the wretched man buried his gold was his fear of punishment – his master was a hard man. This hard master is the voice we carry forward from childhood. Gail Sheehy calls this the "inner custodian". Perhaps there were times when we offered our gold and it was rejected. There are many people who go through the whole education system and are never encouraged to believe they have gold to offer. There are few things more disabling than being made to feel a fool, and the total lack of self-confidence which some people experience is a crushing and stifling block upon any attempts they make to be bold and find some freedom. It should be at the heart of the educational task to lead children and adults out into the use of their own talents and gifts.

We had an interesting and important argument about a training course for lay people in East London. Those organizing the course were divided as to whether on its completion the participants should receive a certificate. The majority said that certification should not be given for completing a course in the Christian faith. The organizing group themselves, like many organizing groups, had already had many many certificates in their lives. Recognition is important. In the completion of the course, one of the greatest satisfactions had been to see people who believed they had little to offer and were often too timid to offer it – for when they had offered it, it had been rejected – discover their confidence and take risks in their lives which they would never have imagined possible. So I believe that midlife, for the person who has grown to maturity with a low opinion of themselves and a deep sense of fear that what they could offer will be rejected as worthless, can be a time of discovering their value as human beings and a life-giving expansion of their interests and commitment.

One of the main sources of a sense of failure is the image of success which is the chosen propaganda of the age. It is hard to fight against the overwhelming pressure of that image. I think that this is where, within ourselves, our resources to tackle deprivation have been undermined. A much-loved mum told me that she remembered at school being so hungry that her tummy made funny rumbling noises. She used to fight during lessons to ensure that her internal emptiness did not become the butt of the other children's wit. Obviously the poverty which caused her tummy to rumble had to be tackled. There was and is an issue of justice which has to be the concern of all. But in one sense, she had developed the resilience to fight it herself. Because so many of us fall such a long way short of the smart set parading their well-being on television and the hoardings, that's no reason for those who have not acquired that life-style to despise themselves or to feel a failure.

The important thing to remember is that to each of us the most lasting values are on offer. Honesty, kindness, patience, tolerance, humour, gentleness, bravery, goodness do not appear in the adverts. "The consumer" is an empty shallow image of the human being. This critique of consumerism is not some fantasy based upon the "the best things in life are free" principle. I enjoy my car and my video too much for that. Nor is it an evasion of the essential battle for more justice in our society – it is rather to say "Don't let them take away your proper self-pride". There is a real dignity in retaining a proper pride in the midst of deprivation. I have seen it in Africa, I have seen it in East London. It would be sad if the propaganda persuaded people that they were helpless and worthless. When I encounter this proper pride, I cherish it and wish to see it more. This doctrine of self-reliance has been used quite cynically as a reason for undermining the welfare state – but that cannot corrupt the virtue itself. There is such a world of difference between a young person who has grown up with or found some personal dignity, whatever the disadvantages of their background, and one who has not. Whether it be through the belief in the dignity of their roots in Africa, or their belonging to a sports team, or in their love of their old Granny, there is in our cities a battle going on for the dignity of our young when so much in society threatens to rob them of it. I believe that one of the signs of this lack of dignity is the ever-ready obscenity on young lips. Somehow the way we use language about the intimate parts of our own bodies and the act of love implies a degeneration of mutual respect. It is commonly said that it's just the way people talk, but the way we talk can, of course, slowly influence the sort of people we are. In my time in East London, I have not found these personal obscenities – depressing as they are – nearly as frightening or depressing as the subtler obscenities uttered by the rich and the powerful in our international society.

So there is a battle for dignity and identity which can reach crisis proportions in midlife, when life has so battered us that we are almost on the edge of giving up altogether. Self-respect cannot be just given back to us by others, it will involve our recognizing that it does not depend upon what or how much we consume, but upon who we are.

But there is an even deeper understanding of failure which is central to the Christian faith. Many of us wrestle through our thirties and forties with great personal problems in marriage, in the battlefield of our own personality, in our families, in our work or lack of work. It looks as though our difficulties are something which have to be gone through. It is part of our own journey and destiny. To the young mother who has multiple sclerosis, the dad who breaks his spine, there is a lifetime of coping with tragedy and insoluble problems. There are many people for whom midlife brings these tragic situations to a head – "life accidents" as Gail Sheehy calls them. There is no longer the optimism of youth, which perhaps for twenty years hopes that things will get better, there is not yet the resolution or resignation of old age. There is only the great burden of Sisyphus, whose punishment was to roll a rock to the top of the hill and yet every time he drew near to the top, it rolled to the bottom again. There can be a sense of despair which says, "I haven't coped with these difficulties by the time I'm forty, which means I never will now. I have the second half of my life still to do carrying the same cross." The question then becomes "How do I tackle the apparently unavoidable suffering by which my life is stained?"

A young doctor said to me, when I was young in faith, that he would never accept a religion of suffering. I had some sympathy with him then, and twenty-four years later I still rebel at the suffering on our planet. I thank God that the Book of Job expresses its awful and inexplicable nature. All the arguing was finished and all the explanations had seemed so feeble in the face of the suffering self, and Job's rebellion only died away when he encountered God:

> Then Job answered the Lord:
> "I know that thou canst do all things
> and that no purpose is beyond thee.
> But I have spoken of great things
> which I have not understood,
> things too wonderful for me to know.
> I knew of thee then only by report,
> but now I see thee with my own eyes.
> Therefore I melt away;
> I repent in dust and ashes."

Job 42:1–6

My doctor friend was not right about the Christian faith, however, because it is not a religion of suffering. We are not expected to choose suffering or lie down under it. We are called to tackle it and to use all our resources to alleviate it and prevent it. Not only does this stem from Christ, who was moved to tackle the suffering which was a way of life for so many people in the Palestine of His time, but also from the Christians in every age who have seen it as their task to continue Christ's work.

But there is no doubt that the Christian revelation can give believers a meaning to their suffering, and suggest ways that it can be embraced and become part of the love of God which saves us. This sprang from the way in which Jesus' suffering was seen to be a promise of paradise. If there is no paradise, God cannot be a God of love, because of the intolerable scope of innocent suffering in our world. But the Christian understanding of suffering is not just a question of heavenly recompense which wipes away all pain in an external dimension of God, it is also a sense of purpose and direction to the endurance of suffering and the struggle to prevent or rectify it. At the heart of the Gospel is a man crying with the heartache of it all. St Paul unravelled the implications of this cross and resurrection of Jesus. He saw that suffering can only be understood in the perspective of eternity.

> For I reckon that the sufferings we now endure bear no comparison with the splendour, as yet unrevealed, which is in store for us.
>
> Romans 8:18

Yet somehow the suffering itself was contained within the universal strategy of God:

> The universe was made the victim of frustration, not by its own choice, but because of him who made it so, yet always there was hope, because the universe itself is to be freed from the shackles of mortality and enter upon the liberty

and splendour of the children of God. Up to the present we know the whole created universe groans in all its parts as if in the pangs of childbirth.

Romans 8:20–22

That image of the pangs of childbirth was a parable of the apparent necessity of the universe to go through pain to come to life. So there is a destiny and a purpose in God's strategy. Not only did Christ's cross act as the turning point, but the crosses which were taken up in following Him were part of the process. This looks like madness to the purely rational man:

> This doctrine of the cross is sheer folly to those who are on their way to ruin, but to us who are on the way to salvation it is the power of God.

1 Corinthians 1:18

This madness, the foolishness of God, is a stumbling block to those who want a solution based on human strength or wisdom. It turns our understanding of failure and weakness upside down.

> Divine folly is wiser than the wisdom of man, and divine weakness stronger than man's strength.

1 Corinthians 1:25

St Paul was able to see that his own suffering was part of the suffering of Christ:

> Wherever we go we carry death with us in our body, the death that Jesus died, that in this body also life may reveal itself, the life that Jesus lives.

2 Corinthians 4:10

In thinking about the person who has to face suffering for the second half of their life, I have used naked theology. I have done so because I believe these things to be true and I have seen them demonstrated in people's lives, but also because I believe there is no other way of saying it. If the midlife crisis is brought to a head because of the realization that certain problems are insoluble, or that certain sufferings will have to be endured, then this Gospel of Hope given to us by God is a way to smile again and begin to tackle life with a renewed meaning.

This, then, offers a way of interpreting our burden, whatever it is. Remarkably, the signs of grace can soon appear. In a way, the heroism of the blitz, and the amazing good cheer of people who emerged from the rubble, provided a living parable. The breakthrough is the realization that in the face of suffering, the way of generous life is the way to find what peace there is. It may have to be for a lifetime, but it also may be that, if we begin to see what is happening to us in the light of Christ, changes in ourselves will take place and motivate changes in others. Our tears and agony of spirit and our searching for God are a sign of God's struggle.

In the same way the Spirit comes to the aid of our weakness. We do not even know how we ought to pray, but through our inarticulate groans the Spirit himself is pleading for us, and God who searches our inmost being knows what the Spirit means, because he pleads for God's people in God's own way; and in everything, as we know, he co-operates for good with those who love God and are called according to his purpose.

Romans 8:26–28

Some of the most creative people I have known in my life have faced up to the suffering their lives contain, somehow seeing a vision of its purpose, and this has turned their life into a treasury for others. These people, from every walk of life, have persuaded me that this foolishness of Christ is the best sense that can be made of life, and is on offer to all.

7

The Person Within

Rewinding the tape of my own life, I can see the repeated signs of an identity struggle. This struggle has made me – is making me – will make me – the person I am. Cared for by loving parents, living in a secure class background, brought up in a beautiful environment, it is still true to say that my life has been a struggle to establish who I am and to find the centre of myself.

Just when I seem to find a resting place, there is a shaking of the foundations, and I have to face a new stage in the battle. Anthony Storr called the goal of this search "the integrity of personality". It is the proper destiny of what is described by the irreplaceable ancient word "soul". If we contemplate for a moment the millions of possible messages stored in our brain, it seems a wonderful miracle that we hold ourselves together at all. A relatively orderly mind and some harmony of thought and feeling are taken for granted, and yet they require an awesome coherence of body, brain and spirit. When I stop and think about this mystery, the fact that the rational human being has developed to the present stage, it reminds me how dependent we are on God, or some unimaginable set of cosmic accidents. It is the grace of one, or incredible coincidences of the other, which has prevented my divided self being a chaotic switchboard or a fractured mind.

I have met many broken or nearly broken people in my life, but I have never felt that they were somehow a different race. Their problems may be greater, their threshold of pain may be lower, but I have so often thought "there but for the grace of God go I". Those who are shipwrecked reveal to the rest of us the dangers of the journey. As Anthony Storr says:

. . . we are all partially neurotic, all, in some degree, less than entirely ourselves.

The difference between people who are sufficiently neurotic to seek, or to need, psychotherapeutic help, and that mysterious being, the "normal" man, is one of degree, not of kind; and there can be no one who has not at times suffered from the inner disharmony which gives rise to neurotic symptoms.

The Integrity of Personality, p.167

Among the clearest demonstrations of our vulnerability are our changes of mood. Some days the world seems to be full of hopeful, kind, beautiful people, and on others of breakages, rows and nasties. It's the same world, and the negative or positive filter is triggered inside me. I suppose there must be some totally serene people in the world, but I haven't yet met them. When I meet a holy person noted for his or her serenity, lo and behold, they have had even worse struggles than I have. Bonhoeffer in prison wrote this:

Who am I? They often tell me
I stepped from my cell's confinement
Calmly, cheerfully, firmly,
Like a squire from his country-house.
Who am I? They often tell me
I used to speak to my warders
Freely and friendly and clearly,
As though it were mine to command.
Who am I? They also tell me
I bore the days of misfortune
Equably, smilingly, proudly,
Like one accustomed to win.

Am I then really all that which other men tell of?
Or am I only what I myself know of myself?
Restless and longing and sick, like a bird in a cage,
Struggling for breath, as though hands were compressing my throat,
Yearning for colours, for flowers, for the voices of birds,
Thirsting for words of kindness, for neighbourliness,

Tossing in expectation of great events,
Powerlessly trembling for friends at an infinite distance,
Weary and empty at praying, at thinking, at making,
Faint, and ready to say farewell to it all?

Who am I? This or the other?
Am I one person today and tomorrow another?
Am I both at once? A hypocrite before others,
And before myself a contemptibly woebegone weakling?
Or is something within me still like a beaten army,
Fleeing in disorder from victory already achieved?

Who am I? They mock me, these lonely questions of
   mine.
Whoever I am, Thou knowest, O God, I am Thine!
　　　　　Letters and Papers from Prison, p.173

Even in this courageous martyr there was uncertainty and
self-doubt. "Am I one person today and tomorrow
another?" Sometimes I feel such a change from moment to
moment. I can often analyse the precise reasons why my
mood changed, when someone said something to encourage
or hurt me, or the lid opened on a can of worms in my area
of responsibility. But sometimes, however hard I search, I
cannot find the trigger of the change, and it is either buried
deeply in my subconscious self, or comes from a source
outside me.

It is not just changes of mood which unsettle me, but also
the battles of conscience. There seems to be one voice inside
my head telling me to do something or not to do something,
and another voice telling me the opposite. If I don't receive
sufficient warning signs before I've done wrong, then I can
be severely punished by feelings of guilt – "bad conscience"
– after I've done it. Within us all, except for the very sick,
there is a battle between right and wrong, however we
describe them. Søren Kierkegaard wrote two parts of a
book. One was called "Either" and the other was called
"Or". There he posed as two different people, who in a

sense represented the two different sides of himself. Whilst we might not be able to express this battle as fully or vividly as a Kierkegaard, we all experience the conflicts.

In my relationships, too, I can feel totally at odds with myself. I may give myself a lecture that the resentment I feel against someone is unjustified or wrong, but the person only needs to appear at my door and inwardly I start sharpening knives. Our relationships help to make us the people we are. The small child beaten and despised by its parents will do serious internal damage to himself, and grow up with scars which can maim him for life in his search to become an integrated and self-assured person. I have seen the frightening disintegration of a mother who, when I first met her, was a cheerful, outgoing and loving person. She moved into a flat which was one of a row of two hundred, without any privacy or space. For various reasons, the people in neighbouring flats disliked her, and she became more and more isolated. Every time she walked out of her door, she came under their scrutiny and criticism. She felt less and less confident to go out at all, and in spite of our efforts to help her come out and join in with life, she slowly cut herself off completely. She went through acute depression and had to be admitted to hospital. Her personality needed human affirmation, and the world became alien to her because she was herself alienated.

R. D. Laing tells the story of a young man called Peter who summed up his fate like this:

> I've been sort of dead in a way. I cut myself off from other people and became shut up in myself. And I can see that you become dead in a way when you do this. You have to live in the world *with* other people. If you don't, something dies inside.
>
> *The Divided Self*, p.133

Disconnection from other human beings, from their affection and energy, leads to a distorted and divided self.

I believe that the development of the individual and the

maturity of his personal relationships proceed hand-in-hand, and that one cannot take place without the other. Self-realization is not an anti-social principle; it is firmly based on the fact that men need each other in order to be themselves, and that those people who succeed in achieving the greatest degree of independence and maturity are also those who have the most satisfactory relationships with others.

Storr, *The Integrity of Personality*, pp.32–33

There is a part in all of us which feels an outsider in some situations. It requires in each of us a special form of courage to turn the key of our prison and reach out to the other human beings around us in love and openness. However much we have been hurt, this way lies our wholeness.

Our sense of alienation, our battles of conscience and our changes of mood are perhaps the most usual ways in which we experience the battle going on inside our personality. For some, the battle leads to a complete split of identity, but for most of us it can cause, from time to time, sadness, guilt or confusion and anxiety. These internal conflicts have been described in many different ways, and the maps of the human personality have changed incredibly in the twentieth century. Just as we must not leave religion and thoughts about God to the professionals, so also we need to try to understand our personality as best we can. Luckily, there are available plenty of attempts to popularize psychology, which can make the mysteries of Freud and Jung and others more accessible to us. Although there are dangers in this process, as there are when everyone is their own theologian, I believe the benefits can be great.

Basically I want to understand as well as I can what makes me think, feel and behave the way I do. When someone hurts me I want to know why, so that I can take steps to heal it. When I keep on getting caught by the same old mistakes, I want to know why and try to find a way of changing. If I can't get on with someone, I want to know why and try to discover ways of getting back on friendly terms with them. I want to struggle out of my worst hang-ups, which do me harm and make life difficult for others. If I can see what makes me react in a particular way, and if I can understand how I've become as I am, then I am starting to have a bit of control over myself and learning which characteristics in myself to strengthen and which to discourage.

The maps seem to look at the divisions, conflicts, sides of personality in three main ways:

1. There is the relationship between the me I know and the me I don't know.
2. There is the tension between my basic instincts and energies and the controls which I try to exercise over them.
3. There is a mixture of persons in me as a result of my experience and relationships.

1. "The me I don't know" is submerged beneath the surface of my conscious mind. My dreams, my memories and many of my thoughts and feelings seem to come from a huge store or factory which keeps on feeding them into my conscious mind. My dreams occur to me whilst I am asleep, and although I often see signs of events that have taken place when awake, they emerge without my conscious instruction. Or again, if my memories can be called up out of the subconscious store into the conscious mind, then that store must include a vast tape library with billions of other tapes that I never consciously play. The changes of mood which can so affect my sense of well-being often come from a source inside myself, but buried out of sight in my subconscious. There can be few who doubt that this "me I don't know" exists.

Because this submerged self is mostly hidden from ourselves, we are sometimes nervous about what is stored there. It may be an unruly and damaging element in our personality, or it could be the source of beautiful imaginings and feelings of peace and ecstasy. With expert help, people are able to bring more and more of this "me I don't know" into the conscious mind to become part of the "me I do know", but even then we have no idea how much still remains concealed. Most of us live in the simple faith that what we don't know can't hurt us, but as soon as we think more seriously about it, we have to recognize that this submerged part of our personality is probably affecting us for good or ill all the time. It may account for our totally surprising reactions or our inexplicable behaviour. It may be the reservoir from which flows the spring of the river of life, or an underground volcano ready to erupt and overwhelm us. It can be a route by which the mystical beauty of God flows into our conscious self, or the source of irrational hatred and fearful fantasy. I shall try to say, in the section on prayer in my last chapter, something about the response of faith to this largely unknown side of ourselves. The Spirit of God is, according to the Christian faith, always waiting and ready to bubble up through this subconscious self. The promise has been made that God's love springs up from inside us, as the water is drawn from a deep well, and what we have to do is draw it up.

2. Another set of maps portray an internal tension between my basic instincts and energies and the control I try to exert over them. The evolutionary description of the origins of man puts human beings firmly in the animal kingdom, with many of the drives and energies of the natural world. For instance, Desmond Morris, in his popular book *The Naked Ape*, claimed that there were three fundamental forms of aggression in animals:

a) to establish a social hierarchy
b) to protect territory
c) to defend the family and the home base

It is not difficult to see that the naked ape is quite keen on all three. If we add other basic drives, such as our need for food, the drive to mate, and the fear for our own safety, we have already described a substantial portion of what makes us human beings. We have all these drives in common with the animal kingdom. But we are also very different from the animals, because of our self-consciousness. We are able to plan, to agonize about the future, to articulate our most intricate thoughts, and to ask questions about the meaning of our lives, etc., etc. From our civilization, our religion, our education, our experience, we develop controls by which we try to reject or accept these basic instincts. Whereas the stag at the rut will fight to gather as many hinds as he can to himself for the mating season, most human beings reject that method of continuing the human race. Whereas the young cuckoo instinctively kicks all the other chicks out of the nest without a qualm of conscience, the human race would either try to resist the temptation to such behaviour or justify it on some spurious moral grounds. The controls come from many sources and instruct us how to behave in our family, our tribe, our society and our world. Sometimes the basic instincts are far stronger than the controls, and sometimes the basic drives and instincts are suppressed by the power of moral controls. Jung described this as a conflict between the natural instinctive man and his self-conscious intellect.

> As long as we are still submerged in nature we are unconscious and we live in the security of instinct . . . It is the growth of consciousness which we must thank for the existence of problems; they are the dubious gift of civilization . . .
>
> It is the sacrifice of the merely natural man – of the unconscious, ingenuous being whose tragic career began with the eating of the apple in Paradise. The biblical fall of man presents the dawn of consciousness as a curse.
>
> *Modern Man in Search of a Soul*, pp.110,111

In the Bible, the result of this "fall" into self-consciousness is a sense of shame, disharmony with nature, suffering and awareness of mortality.

Before Adam and Eve had eaten the apple of the tree of the knowledge of good and evil —

They were both naked, the man and his wife, but they had no feeling of shame towards each other.

> Genesis 2:25

When challenged by God, Adam said to Him:

I heard the sound as you were walking in the garden, and I was afraid because I was naked, and I hid myself.

> Genesis 3:10

God's answer points to Adam's self-awareness as the new element:

Who told you that you were naked? Have you eaten from the tree which I forbade you?

> Genesis 3:11

The after-effect of their disobedience was to bring a life of hardship.

To the woman he said:
"I will increase your labour and your groaning,
and in labour you will bear children . . . "
And to the man he said:
" . . . accursed shall be the ground on your account.
. . . It will grow thorns and thistles for you,
none but wild plants for you to eat.
You shall gain your bread by the sweat of your brow
until you return to the ground;
for from it you were taken.
Dust you are, to dust you shall return."

> Genesis 3:16–19

So man was cut off from his natural relationship with creation.

Although this biblical "fall" is presented as a curse leading to suffering, it is also clear from the account in Genesis that it was the destiny of man to possess the capacity for self-consciousness. God must have known full well that if He put an attractive tree in the garden, with beautiful apples, and strictly forbade human beings to eat them, they would do just that.

This distinction between our animal instinctive nature and our self-conscious intellect and moral controls can sometimes lead to a false view of human nature. It can make people think that the animal instinctive drives are bad and the controls good. But a man or woman who grows up ashamed of their sexuality because they have been taught that sex is wicked, will suffer embarrassment and guilt. On the other hand, a person who, through a damaging life, grows up without any controls on their basic instinctive drives, is a menace. The animal instinctive side of our nature is essential to our humanity, but the mature adult is one who is able to see how that self can be expressed and where it needs to be controlled for his own good and the good of society. We shall see that Jesus and Paul both had something sharp to say about this conflict.

3. If the first two maps describe the way our personality develops by its own intrinsic design, the third is based upon the effect upon our personality of our experience of other people, and especially our closest relationships. In his book *Games People Play*, Eric Berne says that we all carry around in us a "parent", an "adult" and a "child". He calls these characters in our personality "ego states". Our brain and our nervous system are portrayed as being like a computer in which our experience is recorded. The Parent, Child and Adult are

> produced by the playback of recorded events in the past, involving real people, real times, real places, real decisions and real feelings.
>
> *I'm O.K. – You're O.K.*, p.18

In spite of the natural replacement of cells in our brain, the memories we stored as a child are still there. In *I'm O.K. – You're O.K.*, by Thomas Harris, this map is described in more detail. The parent is described as follows:

> In the Parent are recorded all the admonitions and rules and laws that the child heard from his parents and saw in their living. They range all the way from the earliest parental communications interpreted nonverbally through tone of voice, facial expressions, cuddling, or noncuddling, to the more elaborate verbal rules espoused by the parents as the little person became able to understand words. In this set of recordings are the thousands of "nos" directed at the toddler, the repeated "don'ts" that bombarded him, the looks of pain and horror in mother's face when his clumsiness brought shame on the family . . . Likewise are recorded the coos of pleasure of a happy mother and the looks of delight of a proud father.
>
> *I'm O.K. – You're O.K.*, p.20

In children we often hear echoes of their parents talking. Children can't help but build their character in part on their relationship with their mother and father, who for a time have such great power over them. Their wishes, their anger, their love are an all-important facet of our lives. The "parent" in us is thought of as playing a rather dominating, moral teacher and watchdog part, and many people live under this shadow in a way which constantly denies their value. They are forever apologizing, forever calling themselves inadequate, forever condemning themselves for the poverty and sinfulness of their performance. On the other hand, it is also frightening to see the person who has killed off the cautionary parent and lives out a dangerous amoral alienation in society.

The "child" in us, on the other hand, tends to reproduce not the parental attitudes, but the feelings of the child itself, when it was frightened, lost or frustrated, as well as the positive, inquisitive, fun side of childhood. There are things that can happen to us today which re-create the situation of childhood and bring on the same feelings we felt then. Frequently we may find ourselves in situations where we are faced with impossible alternatives, where we find ourselves in a corner, either actually, or in the way we see it. These "hook" the Child, as we say, and cause a replay of the original feelings of frustration, rejection, or abandonment, and we relive a latter-day version of the small child's primary depression. Therefore, when a person is in the grip of feelings, we say his Child has taken over. When his anger dominates his reason, we say his Child is in command.

There is a bright side too! In the Child is also a vast store of positive data. In the Child reside creativity, curiosity, the desire to explore and know, the urges to touch and feel and experience, and the recordings of the glorious, pristine feelings of first discoveries. In the Child are recorded the countless, grand a-ha experiences, the firsts in the life of the small person, the first drinking from the garden hose, the first stroking of the soft kitten, the first sure hold on mother's nipple, the first time the lights go on in response to his flicking a switch, the first submarine chase of the bar of soap, the repetitious going back to do these glorious things again and again. The feelings of these delights are recorded too.

ibid., pp.26–27

The "adult" in a person begins to develop as soon as they begin to take their own steps and are no longer completely dependent. From ten months onwards the child becomes mobile and starts exercising his own choices, exploring and checking out his parents' view of his world. From being a fragile and tentative "ego state", with proper encouragement and growing independence and confidence, the adult develops.

Through the Adult the little person can begin to tell the difference between life as it was taught and demonstrated to him (Parent), life as he felt it or wished it or fantasied it (Child), and life as he figures it out by himself (Adult).

The Adult is a data-processing computer, which grinds out decisions after computing the information from three sources: the Parent, the Child, and the data which the Adult has gathered and is gathering. One of the important functions of the Adult is to examine the data in the Parent, to see whether or not it is true and still applicable today, and then to accept it or reject it; and to examine the Child to see whether or not the feelings there are appropriate to the present or are archaic and in response to archaic Parent data. The goal is not to do away with the Parent and Child but to be free to examine these bodies of data.

ibid., p.30

How these three characters in one person operate together in each of us makes up the sort of individual we are and influences the way we conduct ourselves in our relationships. In the book I've just mentioned, there are many examples of how the analysis can help us understand why we are behaving and feeling as we do. What triggered my depressed feelings when my wife was not there to cook my supper? It was obviously the Child in me, needing the security I had drawn from my mother always being there at the same vulnerable time of day. Why did I get angry when my fifteen-year-old daughter answered me back when I thought I had made a clear and indisputable ruling? It was because she was claiming the rights of her Adult, who no longer saw Dad's word as final! Why do I find it so difficult to say "no"? It is because inside me I feel I'm never going to "do it right", and I need the approval of others. The Adult tells me I am not Atlas trying to take on the whole world. The Child in me, I hope, stops me getting too pompous and encourages me to enjoy playing.

Once the broad outline of the map is understood, it can illuminate and unravel whole areas of bad feelings and can restore to a person their own adult self. All sorts of questions like these become more acute in our middle years, in our relationships, in our roles in life, and in our self-understanding. Because they reflect the Parent/Child in us, it can be illuminating in understanding the way we cope with authority.

Why does he always make me feel useless and inadequate?
Why do I become so nervous when I have to make decisions or speak in public?
Why do I speak to my boss in such a patronizing way?
Why do I have to disagree with everything my boss says?
Why does that junior colleague bring out the worst in me?

It is possible to unravel many of the sources of our anger, our depressed feelings and our resentments. In the sequel, *Staying O.K.*, Amy and Thomas Harris recommend a process of Trackdown (pp.71–82) – when our feelings take a plunge, they suggest a little self-examination, carefully staged to try to discover what hurts, what caused the hurt and how it can be dealt with.

These are some of the many maps available. They are all limited because they are trying to describe the profound mystery of our personality. Thomas Harris writes:

We are deeply indebted to Freud for his painstaking and pioneering efforts to establish the theoretical foundation upon which we build today. Through the years, the scholars have elaborated, systematized, and added to his theories. Yet the "persons within" have remained elusive, and it seems that the hundreds of volumes which collect dust and the annotations of psychoanalytic thinkers have not provided adequate answers to the persons they are written about.

I'm O.K. – You're O.K., p.2

"The persons within have remained elusive" – and it looks as though none of the maps is adequate in itself – though they each offer some vision and self-understanding. None of the maps gives us the right to say we "know" an individual, or ourselves for that matter.

In spite of their usefulness, many of the maps appear to contain a serious flaw. They give largely negative accounts of the effects of religion on the personality, often portraying belief in God as having either harmful effects upon people, or at least halting the development and maturity of the adult self. Gail Sheehy, for instance, in her book *Passages*, refers to religion only twice. In both cases the person concerned found their adult freedom by throwing off their parents' religious inheritance.

Much of this negative attitude towards faith seems to derive from Freud's critique of religion, stoked by suspicion of the direction the Christian religion often appears to be taking in the United States. In his book *Freud and Christianity* (p.73), R. S. Lee says this:

> Freud says that the Super-ego is the seat of religion, and there is much truth in his contention. But he bases this assertion on the conception of religion that is not adequate to describe the Christian life and he so blandly ignores the vast amount of scientific, historical study that has been devoted to the sources of Christianity, that his conception is scarcely worth calling even a travesty of it.

Christianity would seem to be portrayed either as the result of the overbearing "Parent" of God the Father, or the product of the wish-fulfilment of the "Child" in ourselves. It is not difficult to see both these effects in individual Christians. The idea of God can certainly feature in our personality as a grim, judgemental, punitive, totally demoralizing and humourless judge, reducing us to frightened, guilt-ridden, narrowed-down people – "miserable offenders" who are afraid of being human, who bury their potential and kill off the child in them. Dominated by such a fearful God, a person has to become self-righteous or live a double life. The hypocrites were the mask-wearers who may have fooled the people, but certainly didn't fool God. Also, our understandable fear of the world, our loneliness, our despair, can make us crave for the security of a heavenly Father who must then, once created, remain in the kindly image in which we have made Him. There is obviously a drive within us which grows out of our need to have a heavenly father and mother who will not have all the unreliability, instability, impotence and failings of our earthly parents. Both the servile and the infantile approaches to God from time to time damage individual Christians and the Church, but from earliest times there has been a call to maturity and adult responsibility, and also the good news that God is greater than the fearful tyrant created by our guilt and inadequacy.

Jesus said to Mary in the Garden of Gethsemane, when she threw herself in dependence upon Him:

> Do not cling to me.
>
> John 20:17

When Jesus left His disciples to go to be with God, He returned their responsibility to them.

> I call you servants no longer; a servant does not know what his master is about. I have called you friends.
>
> John 15:15

And there can be few more direct appeals to the adult or the ego or the soul than:

> Love one another as I have loved you.
>
> John 15:12

We are not called to infantile dependence.

St Paul experienced Christ as freeing him from the perpetual harassment of his super-ego – the "Parent" inculcated into his personality by the law was necessary, but was a permanent threat to his freedom.

Therefore the law [meaning the Jewish Law, the Torah] is

in itself holy and the commandment is holy and just and good.

Romans 7:12

But his encounter with God in Christ freed him from the dictatorship of the law and opened up for him the adult citizenship of the free man:

Christ set us free, to be free men. Stand firm, then, and refuse to be tied to the yoke of slavery again.

Galatians 5:1

Obviously many Jews would not accept St Paul's interpretation of the Torah, but my point is that the first great Apostle to the Gentiles experienced Christ as a new freedom from the old judging parent within. He would endorse this from *Staying O.K.* (p.132):

A favourite scripture of mine is found in 1 John: "If our heart condemn us, God is greater than our heart and knows all things"; I am only human, imperfect, forgiven and loved anyway. Amazing relief: God and the Parent are not the same.

The result was that Paul could embrace his own adult future and was offered a way to maturity and integrity:

So shall we all at last attain to the unity inherent in our faith and our knowledge of the Son of God – to mature manhood, measured by nothing less than the full stature of Christ.

Ephesians 4:13

That's some stature!

With the coming of Christ, man's picture of the ancient, primitive, aweful God was seen in a new light. There was a new dispensation which called mankind to walk tall.

Remember where you stand: not before the palpable, blazing fire of Sinai, with the darkness, gloom, and whirlwind, the trumpet-blast and the oracular voice, which they heard, and begged to hear no more; for they could not bear the command, "If even an animal touches the mountain, it must be stoned." So appalling was the sight, that Moses said, "I shudder with fear."

No, you stand before Mount Zion and the city of the living God, heavenly Jerusalem, before myriads of angels, the full concourse and assembly of the first-born citizens of heaven, and God the judge of all, and the spirits of good men made perfect . . .

Hebrews 12:18–23

God is love, and love casts out fear. In this love of God there is "a judgement", there is "a way" to live, there is an awesome mystery, but God has declared Himself to be on our side and freed us to live our lives to the full, taking responsibility for the world He has given us. Bonhoeffer captured the spirit of the call to adult life in his "Stations on the Road to Freedom". The journey described involves the development of a mature self in the love of God:

O freedom, long have we sought thee in discipline and in action and in suffering. Dying, we behold thee now, and see thee in the face of God.

Letters and Papers from Prison, p.162

What Freud and others have failed to see is that the God many of us have discovered is like the loving father and mother who want nothing more for their children than that they should become mature, loving human beings, pouring their love and faith and hope into the common weal. It is a mistake we often make that when we criticize other people's belief and ideology, we compare our own best understanding of our own belief with the worst examples of theirs! Christians have excelled at this sleight of hand in treating other religions and ideologies. But it is as foolish, because religion is often perverted, for the non-believers to close their eyes to its great truth, as it is absurd for Christians to ignore the essential secular insights which have transformed our understanding of the human personality and the universe. As R. S. Lee gently remarked,

> Atheism will . . . tend to betray its infantile origin by its preoccupation in a negative way with the idea of God.
> *Freud and Christianity*, p.125

It is just as possible for a person to eliminate God through illusion and wish-fulfilment and fear as it is to create Him. A map which excludes the reality of God is like a chart which omits to mark the sea. To my view, so many of the needs and hunger and trauma described in the case studies from which the maps are drawn, are signs of the omission of God from the scene. I am not producing God out of a hat to solve life's problems like a magician, rather like those who say: "Harrow your hearers until they are well and truly frightened and depressed and then bring out your Christ", nor am I trying to calculate some sort of equation in which, by amazing coincidence, X = Christ, but rather to talk about the Christian vision of man in its attempts to unravel "the person within". I believe it is an interpretation which still has a great deal to offer believer and non-believer alike, and provides a map worthy of study, and it is to that that I now turn.

8

Struggling with Faith

So far, I have looked at our middle years from the starting point of our experience – the ageing process, the generation trap, our relationships and our personality. Now I want to concentrate on the insights of faith. I have said that, whilst the secular creeds are important and have much to offer, their repeated negative view of faith means they tend to cut human beings off from the great resources of God. Before I try to say what clues the Christian faith offers, there is a warning. Faith is so often produced as if by magic. It is as though Jesus, when offering us "the Way, the Truth and the Life", allowed us to opt out of the pain of life. Many Christians seem to claim to have solved life's mysteries. They are not at all convincing – because the rest of us know the mysteries are alive and well and giving us a lot of trouble. Jesus did not offer answers which, once we know them, absolve us from life's difficulties, rather He often spoke in frightening paradox – we have to lose our lives to find them. Although He did not survive into mid-life, it is a comfort to me that He saw with human eyes, heard with human ears, felt with a human heart, thought with a human brain, and most certainly had an identity crisis of His own. Faith is not a solution to life, it is a way of living it. Faith does not free us from perplexity, or even our share of the agony, it rather affirms the meaning of our life and, through the struggle, gives us some assurance of God with us in the middle of all that mess. Faith does not by-pass human destiny, it opens wider and offers us abundant life. Abundant life does not mean trouble-free, painless, anodyne life, it means life lived to the full, sharing its mysteries, its agony and its beauty. So when we search for the clues of faith, we are not likely to find large doses of serenity (though I hope we shall find some); we shall find the inner courage and love necessary to face the future in the way Christ would have us travel.

My mother recently gave me all the letters I had written to her and my father in my mid-twenties. They cover the time of my first becoming a Christian when I was an accountant and then doing my National Service. Reading these letters again, I was shocked by their arrogance. At that time, I was obviously overwhelmed by the experience of conversion, and I now flinch when I recognize the prig who appears there. I was so convinced of the simple truth I possessed. I used to give good, uplifting, Christian advice to my parents, and I was obviously quite proud of my fasting one day a week and the clarity with which I saw life. It is not surprising that a young man who had had a dramatic religious experience should feel that he was God's answer, not only to his mother and father, but quite a chunk of the known world!

But my certainty did not last long. As I began to share that faith, to worship in church and to pray, and as I found myself struggling with life without access to easy solutions, it felt very different. My image of the Christian was of someone who took on life more vividly, with greater knowledge and assurance, but sometimes in the church I felt as though I was putting on a strait-jacket which would somehow make me less human, and certainly cut me off from my friends, who thought the whole thing was a bit odd. I found that there were quite a few Christians who seemed to be trying to escape reality into a closed, ecclesiastical ghetto. There were, however, plenty who encouraged me to believe I could be fully human and Christian. How could God, I asked myself, possibly want me in His name to become a "holier than thou" prig who could have little or no relationship with the "ordinary" people whom I loved and treasured? If those were the "out" people, then I thought I'd rather be "out" than "in". So at university I threw myself into the "worldly" side, and hoped and prayed that I'd find God there as well.

It was at this nervous point, when I wondered how the Church could respond to Jesus' warning that the harlots and sinners went into the kingdom of God first, that I read Dietrich Bonhoeffer's *Letters and Papers from Prison*. It was a moment of revelation for me. Bonhoeffer was a theologian who resisted the Nazis. He was teaching in the USA and was invited to stay and criticize Germany from the outside. But he decided that his Christian discipleship as a German demanded that he return to Germany. He was imprisoned for his part in the conspiracy to assassinate Hitler, and in the end, at the age of 39, just before the end of the war in 1945, he was executed. In his prison, he was exposed to humanity in the raw, and had to find God without the presence of the visible Church. In that experience he rediscovered that faith is a way of living in God's world and "drinking its cup to the lees" for God's sake. He did not say, in the face of his suffering, "stop the world, I want to get off". Nor did he deny the importance of the Church which he loved. Rather he recognized that the Church – the Christian – must be truly incarnate – fully human, sharing totally in the world's life like Christ. His was not an uncritical approval of the world – as a lover of his country he was against everything it stood for in those terrible years – but rather a costly sharing in the storms of the human conscience and the tears of things.

I, like many others, had to learn that faith was not a way of escape, nor a crib sheet for life's exams, nor a box of magical tricks. It has to be lived out in the world's canteen, in the pub, at the market, in the recording studios, in the board-room, in the House of Commons. It is to be discovered in the main stream of life, not in a religious backwater.

One of the stories told in Father Anthony de Mello's *The Song of the Bird* (p.60) makes the point:

River Water for Sale

> The master's sermon that day consisted
> of one enigmatic sentence.
>
> With a wry smile he said, "All
> I do is sit by the bank of the river,
> selling river water."

I was so busy buying the water that I failed to see the river.

God's life is mid-stream in His world. We find it as we look for His kingdom on earth. For this reason, it cannot be just a question of my own individual salvation. It involves the well-being of the whole community.

My time as a priest and a Bishop in East London has made me realize that justice and the healthy society are not just a matter of changing individuals, we also have to tackle the great structures which control so much of our life. The Church, through laity and clergy, must not isolate herself behind the walls of ecclesiastical busyness, but must be involved corporately in the great social issues such as housing, employment, race etc., which have a profound spiritual reality. We cannot hide in our individualistic idea of salvation – "I'm saved – let the devil take the rest." We have to work out our salvation in the real world, where multi-nationals, the borough councils, the governments, the police, the military, have such a massive influence on the way we live. This has been the constant theme of our recent battles as the Church in society. In this country, religion has been seen mostly as a matter for the individual, and this dichotomy between private and public life has allowed some Christians to keep their Sunday worship and their working life in two separate worlds. This is a sort of split personality which is bad news for the Church and bad news for the world. We need a greater sense of our corporate responsibility. The Christian faith is a challenge to individualism.

For Christ is like a single body with its many limbs and organs, which, many as they are, together make up one body. . . .

But God has combined the various parts of the body, giving special honour to the humbler parts, so that there might be no sense of division in the body, but that all its organs might feel the same concern for one another. If one organ suffers, they all suffer together. If one flourishes, they all rejoice together.

1 Corinthians 12:12,24–26

Yet it can also be rightly argued that the sickness of society
is due to the spiritual lethargy of the individuals who belong
to it. It was Jung who wrote:

> It is, unfortunately, only too clear that if the individual is
> not truly regenerated in spirit, society cannot be either,
> for society is the sum total of individuals in need of
> redemption . . . and the salvation of the world consists in
> the salvation of the Individual Soul.
>
> *The Undiscovered Self*, pp.56–57

The Bible combines the corporate and the individual salvation in a way which can hold these two sides of our life
together. Just as we are told about belonging to one Body,
so also each individual human being is a wonderful mystery
known and valued by God. The psalmist says to God:

> Thou it was who didst fashion my inward parts;
> thou didst knit me together in my mother's womb.
> I will praise thee, for thou dost fill me with awe;
> wonderful thou art, and wonderful thy works.
> Thou knowest me through and through:
> my body is no mystery to thee,
> how I was secretly kneaded into shape
> and patterned in the depths of the earth.
> Thou didst see my limbs unformed in the womb,
> and in thy book they are all recorded;
> day by day they were fashioned,
> not one of them was late in growing.
> How deep I find thy thoughts, O God,
> how inexhaustible their themes!
>
> Psalm 139:13–17

> What is man that thou shouldst remember him,
> mortal man that thou shouldst care for him?

Yet thou hast made him little less than a god,
crowning him with glory and honour.

Psalm 8:4–5

Whether they are kings or beggars, in the Bible they are all individuals, and yet, whether they are kings or beggars, they are all part of the community of God's people, essential to the whole.

Every individual pours his or her life into the reservoir of human experience. Each person has a value and significance, and, for good or ill, moves the human race a fraction towards our goal. Each of us is related to others, each of our actions ripples out through the rings of our own pool and affects others. The change of an individual can change society – we can create faith, hope and love – or their opposites. I want to say that it is profoundly important that each of us works out who we are, and what we will contribute to the human story. We have seen in the mass rallies of the Third Reich how evil individuals can gather to themselves all the latent terrifying nastiness of the human crowd, and mobilize the mob and the nation to acts of incredible bestiality. It is also true that we have seen individuals who have, from the most unlikely beginnings, by their own human being, mobilized and strengthened the best in the people around them. Some of the most influential people in my life would never have thought of themselves in that way: a cockney woman who nurses severely handicapped children; a politician who maintained his integrity under the gravest personal risk; a taxi-driver who became a philosopher in his cab-seat; a hard-pressed mum of six; an idealistic young man who reminded me of the hope I had; a person of quiet prayer; a business man standing up for his faith – they have all made a profound difference to my life, and, I guess, to the lives of many others.

Some of the most prophetic literature of our century has rightly warned against the denial of individual significance. Whether it be the importance of Winston Smith's battle to be an individual against the totalitarian spying eye of Big Brother in *1984*, or the Savage in *Brave New World* revealing the profundity of the human struggle against the anaesthetized Brave New World. Whether it is Dr Zhivago pursuing his personal love against the tide of massive social change, or Charlie Chaplin swallowed up by the great machine of technological advance and somehow surviving and refusing to be just a cog. Or the frightening scenes in Chinese mental hospitals where dissidents are regularized, and the "one who flew over the cuckoo's nest" purchasing by his death the freedom of one of his friends from being an electrified and medicated zombie. In all these stories we see a battle for the destiny and dignity of the individual human being.

Yet we seem to let so much of our lives go to waste, without the sharpened awareness of our potential and our real worth. I don't know whether our spiritual lethargy is caused by comfortable self-centredness or a sense of impotence.

Recently I heard an expert on ants talking about their community. Apparently, if an ant is dying, it gives off a special chemical which tells other worker ants that it has to be carried to their cemetery. I had to kill a group of ants which were invading our kitchen. One ant survived but she would have been better dead, because she then dashed in total panic from corpse to corpse, totally unable to respond to the fearful smell of death. As we watch the starving in Ethiopia, the villages destroyed by cyclones in Bangladesh, the earthquake in Mexico, the ashen faces of young drug addicts, the amoral eyes of alienated people, the endless circles of violence, we sometimes feel like that helpless ant. Anyone who has looked at the human debris of Auschwitz or Hiroshima, and taken on board some of the appalling predictions for spaceship earth, must feel on the edge of their own stability. What is so amazing – but perhaps it is a sensible defensive measure – is the way we manage to shut all this away and confine it to news bulletins, meanwhile proceeding with life almost as though nothing had happened, until it happens to us. But it is happening to us, because we are not just part of one family, one town or one nation, but also part of one race. We are all bound together in our little world. Our security and wealth are intimately related to the insecurity, poverty and violence "out there".

The poor ant felt impotent when faced with all her dead

sisters (only the females seem to work!), and in our time there is a very considerable sense of impotence threatening us as individuals. There is a great deal of shrugging of the shoulders, opting out, a lethargy caused by the feeling that we can't change anything. We can vote, but even that seems such a minimal influence – especially if your political party has no power. Maybe this feeling of helplessness combines with the comfortable life-style to lull us to sleep.

We need to wake up and say, "I am important – whoever I am." If we, as individuals, do not recognize and embrace our destiny, then our shadow disappears.

So this self of mine, these selves of ours, have to find a way of being the unique, whole human person we can be – both in the face of a bewildering and often frightening external world, and in the crucible of our own personal inward being. Our midlife is a key time in this personal journey, because it not only prepares us for middle age and old age, but also is the time when most of us can make or mar our contribution to our world. We can either become more truly ourselves, or lose our individuality in uncritical, conformist reactions. Jung called it a setting-out on the second journey, and there is a sense in which it is the turn of the rudder that sets the course for our ultimate destination, and it is therefore important to have some idea of where we are heading.

In his book *The Creation of Consciousness* (p.9), Edward F. Edinger says this:

> History and anthropology teach us that a human society cannot long survive unless its members are psychologically contained within a central living myth. Such a myth provides the individual with a reason for being. To the ultimate questions of human existence it provides answers which satisfy the most developed and discriminating members of the society.

Our society has no "central living myth". We are a multi-cultural community with many myths. There is a rich store to explore, but we find it hard to discover a unity of purpose. In our confusion, bad myths seem easier to grow – like weeds in the garden – and they divide and degrade the spirit. The fascination with the occult both corrupts and threatens those who indulge in it. We see on the fringes of the Church how destructive can be the mythology of demons and evil spirits literally translated into our contemporary world. We still see around us in East London, young people whose personalities are hardened and brutalized by the Nazi myth. The "class war" interpretation of contemporary Britain does real damage to the reality of our complex social relationships. The deifying of "Market Forces" frequently baptizes amoral social planning and hallows greed. The myth of white superiority leads to the insulting and dangerous racial undercurrents in all strata of our society, and has made it possible for bad law to be put on the statute book. Both religion and secular myths can enter the soul of society and change its character and direction. We shall perhaps make progress when we have found ways of encouraging the good plants to grow and leave less space for the weeds to take root. By the terrible conflict of the Second World War, a great evil was defeated, but it left a lot of people in a spiritual void. A spiritual void sucks in bad spirits. I do not believe we shall find a "central living myth", but rather have to learn to discern good from bad and find a mutual understanding and respect which allow the good to prevail and enrich our community. The Christian faith makes universal claims, but is neither the sole source of the vision of God, nor the whole wisdom about man. Although we believe our faith is "the" faith, we must recognize the exciting challenge of the other faiths held and believed by the world at our door.

Faith, then, is not a means of evading the pressures of the world, nor does it provide a safe box full of neat solutions; it is rather a living relationship between God and us. It is like trusting our father to hold us when we are learning to swim. It is like walking by a cliff when we can't see, being led by the hand. It is like being in a whole heap of trouble, but somehow trusting that a way through will be found. It is like sharing in a human tragedy and finding some hope in it. Faith is like being happy – you're not sure why or how, but you just are. It is like staying with the unpopular solution because you believe it is right. There are so many sides to faith, because it expresses the relationship of the whole of our life to God.

It is a sad thought that for a vast number of people in our society, the word "God" is almost empty. The ways in which God used to occur in ordinary thinking and talking have been reduced, so that for many people the only time they use His name is to swear, or to marry, or to bury someone. But then, even God was declared to be dead! If God is true and the maker of the universe, then all people are in fact relating to Him through their very existence, their breathing and speaking and feeling and thinking, even though they don't use the name of God to describe that relationship. Faith does not accept that we are all here through some great cosmic accident, but that all things come to be through the life, energy and love of God.

In faith we grow to see the universe as filled with the being of God, to see our own small earth as alive with the outpouring of God, and to see people as the children of God. It is not easy, however, to communicate this faith in today's world, because so many people have both abandoned or never known the stories by which it was conveyed, and also find it so difficult to think and feel God. Although the faith-filled person is the best communication of the truth by which he lives, it is necessary also to talk about God, to reveal the source of the strength. To talk about God is to try to cross dimensions – from the dimension of our time and our space to the dimension of God. Although in faith we may feel we can sometimes cross that bridge, it is much more difficult to help others to cross it. For Christians, Jesus is the main bridge between our human understanding and God. What God has always been and always will be, in so far as that can be demonstrated in a human life, was demonstrated in Jesus. But even Jesus had difficulty in communicating God to those who were closed in their minds:

Eyes have they but they see not; ears have they but they hear not.

Mark 8:18

His most usual way was to tell parables:

> How shall we picture the kingdom of God, or by what parable shall we describe it? It is like the mustard seed, which is smaller than any seed in the ground at its sowing. But once sown, it springs up and grows taller than any other plant, and forms branches so large that the birds can settle in its shade.

> Mark 4:30–32

"God is like a person who . . . ", "Heaven is like a place where . . ." So through parables He took the experiences that people knew in their everyday lives and used them to describe the purpose and nature of God. But He did not just tell parables, He also drew upon the faith handed down to Him as a Jew, sometimes accepting its teaching without amendment, sometimes transforming it, sometimes giving it a new set of priorities. Indeed, for the Christian the story of faith begins with the faith of the people of Israel. On the basis of God's covenant with them, the Jews have built their identity and their purpose. To share in their worship at home or in the synagogue is to see the continuing influence of their inheritance of faith on their struggle in the world. Their faith goes on, the Passover is celebrated, the stories of their faith are retold.

Indeed, the Bible is a library of books about the human identity crisis. This library does not present us with a totally consistent, carefully worked out theory. Instead, we see a pageant of people, ideas, dreams, history, philosophy, poetry and fable. As someone said, "The whole of human life is there." I would be suspicious of anyone who produced from its pages a neatly developed highway code for our personality. Yet patterns emerge and, as we get steeped in it, we can sense we are at the heart of the human struggle and looking in a mirror of our own soul.

It begins with the identity crisis of humankind in Adam, then wrestles with the destiny of God's chosen people, Israel, and ends with a new beginning through Christ. The identity crisis is seen primarily in terms of our relationship to God. This is not the question of one-eighth of ourselves which is commonly called "religious", but eight-eighths of ourselves, because God is the source of all our being.

Gail Sheehy commented from her experience of other people's crises:

> Many people locked in early to a tight religious tradition find themselves struggling by midlife against absolutist positions that no longer correspond to their experience.
>
> *Passages*, p.133

That is true, and can lead to a deeper and more personal journey with God. It is also true that many people in midlife discover the hollow sound of their secular certainties, and feel highly dissatisfied with the goals and objectives which they sought in their youth with total enthusiasm and commitment. Midlife can be a time for searching for something more to life, which can be a sign of the desire for God. It is a good time to renew a stagnant faith, to open up or to discover a new one.

Perhaps the character in the Old Testament who can encourage us most in this journey is Abraham, the father of faith – his life was one long identity crisis. It is an encouragement that the father of the multitudes, the friend of God, should stumble from crisis to crisis. His story portrays the man of faith. He trusts God up to a point, but then doubts God's reliability and begins to make his own plans. God seemed to test him to see how far he would go in faith. He was uprooted from his homeland by God's command:

> Leave your country, your kinsmen and your father's house and go to a country that I will show you.
>
> *Genesis 12:1*

He and his wife Sarah were still childless beyond the time of childbearing, yet God promised:

> I will make you into a great nation, I will bless you and make your name great.
>
> Genesis 12:2

The narrator, in telling the story of Abraham, calls the reader to faith and obedience. He tells us to trust God and respond to His calling, and then we shall find our true destiny – the impossible will become possible. If we lose trust through doubt or cynicism, and we anxiously start to plan solutions based solely on our own strength, we are quickly in trouble. Sometimes we trust in God who gives us the courage to decide or enables us to cope with the impossible, and sometimes we grow anxious, stay awake all night, try to manipulate our lives, and so plunge ourselves and others into misery. This is why faith is such a mobilizing facet of our personality. It is not an indemnity against risk, but it creates an attitude of mind which enables us to act in an adult way.

> By faith Abraham obeyed the call to go out to a land destined for himself and his heirs, and left home without knowing where he was to go.
>
> Hebrews 11:8

People who do not believe in God often cannot understand how faith can enhance our humanness. They often suggest that it is just blind faith, or an opting out of the tests and pitfalls of our lives. Yet to live through faith in the God you love, is an emancipating experience because it releases you from the worst anxiety and gives you the courage to set out "without knowing where you are to go".

Midlife is a time when faith is of the greatest importance, and yet it is so often a missing ingredient. Abraham was called to set out on a journey without security and not seeing the destination. For some people in midlife there has to be a change of direction – with all its anxiety. We worry about how things are going to turn out, we can't make decisions and keep getting caught between several options. On the other hand, when it is clear that we've got to stay where we are, and we can't see much in it for us, then faith in God is still important. It can shift the self-pity and the resentment and open up the possibilities we hadn't dreamt of, where we are. Faith has even managed to turn prison into a place of hope and creative opportunity. If we feel dragged down by our personality as it has developed so far, by habit or guilt or failure, then faith can be just that offer of hope that we can change. Abraham is such an encouragement because through faith he keeps on coming back. God had made a promise to him, and however often Abraham turned away and made a fool of himself, he could come back and say to God, "Well, that's my way – now let's try yours."

Faith can release us from the tremendous self-concern which is such a feature of our midlife doldrums. God has promised to us, as to Abraham, the life that is right and good for us, and we shall find it by trusting in Him. The brakes are taken off and we can move forward. Using Kierkegaard's parable we launch out in an ocean over seventy thousand fathoms. One of the modern parables of faith which makes the same point is free fall from a plane. As a vertigo victim, it is a parable I hope I shall have to accept only at second hand, but it seems to be a marvellous expression of freedom, and it is all based upon faith that the 'chute will open and carry the flyer safely to earth. Faith in God is not a reduction of our adulthood, it is the means by which we can find the courage to be, to trust people and commit ourselves to open living. So many times we feel bruised and hurt by experience, and we are tempted to turn in on ourselves and not risk the same thing happening again. So often I have seen in myself and watched in the eyes of others, the tight self-concern of anxiety. Faith encourages us to put our worry in its place and to trust that a way will be found. God is calling me to be positive, to take the risk, to forget myself, to trust that all will be well. Faith is discovering in the risks we take, in the commitment we give, that God's love is at the heart of all things. Faith is not a once-for-all escape from the tension of being, but rather an invitation to travel. For this reason, the Christian is involved up to his neck in the drama of the human spirit – not as someone who has pat, ready-made answers, but searching for the will of God. Faith does not exempt us from crying, bleeding and suffering. We may not enter into the human debate and the agonies of our world as though we are protected by a spiritual disinfectant. We follow a Lord who drank deep of the world's agony. The writer to the Hebrews says of Abraham:

> He was looking forward to the city with firm foundations whose architect and builder is God.
>
> Hebrews 11:10

There is a sense in which faith helps us look forward – gives us a future. Nothing could be more important to our generation, overshadowed by the threat of possible nuclear annihilation.

> Faith gives substance to our hopes and makes us certain of realities we do not see.
>
> Hebrews 11:1

This faith is free, but not cheap. It involves us in real decisions about ourselves, and it involves us in facing up to God in our life. Because we remain ourselves and because in our personality many tapes have been played and many more are stored, the journey of faith will often see us struggling with God. There is a story told about Abraham's grandson, Jacob. He had run away from home after cheating his brother out of his birthright. He had been away many years, and was now returning with his family and flocks. He was afraid of facing up to his brother Esau, and he spent the night by himself in preparation. During the night

> . . . a man wrestled with him there till daybreak. When the man saw that he could not throw Jacob, he struck him in the hollow of his thigh, so that Jacob's hip was

165

dislocated as they wrestled. The man said, "Let me go, for day is breaking", but Jacob replied, "I will not let you go unless you bless me." He said to Jacob, "What is your name?", and he answered, "Jacob." The man said, "Your name shall no longer be Jacob, but Israel, because you strove with God and with men, and prevailed."

Genesis 32:24–28

He wrestled with God. That is almost inevitable in the journey of faith, because it is a relationship between God, immense and free and holy, and human beings struggling with mortality. Jacob's struggling with God taught him who he was, and brought about reconciliation with his brother, who responded with forgiveness:

Jacob then went on ahead . . . bowing low to the ground seven times as he approached him. Esau ran to meet him and embraced him; he threw his arms round him and kissed him, and they wept.

Genesis 33:3–4

9

Defining Love

In our middle years, we lay the foundations of the second half of our life. It is a decisive time. It can be a time when we make new choices and set out to change the way we look at things, and sometimes alter the pattern of life itself. The steps to be taken require faith, whether that faith is drawn from believing we can do it on the basis of our own resources, or from our relationship with God. If we are searching for God, then it is important to recognize that the experience will be different from simply being answerable to ourselves. Because we want to take God into account, then we are not simply setting our own goals, asserting our own values, seeking fulfilment on our own terms. This is a hard nettle to grasp, and one whose sting turns people away. But making the choices, the changes, the breaking of habits, on our own strength alone is also hard. To give up smoking, to give up security, to be reconciled to someone we hate, or to tackle some self-defeating habit, require of us a powerful exercise of will – not just once, but often over and over again.

If we are looking for God, then we are no longer self-contained. Our life comprises our own self, our own self in relation to others and our own self in relation to God. But to relate to someone, we need to know what they are like – or at least to know enough to make and sustain the relationship. God, in spite of all His communications with the human race, through messengers and inspirations, remains invisible. It is impossible to imagine a way that God could be visible if He is the ground of all being. In our dimension, the immense Goodness of God cannot appear. Many of us have sung since we were children:

> Immortal, invisible, God only wise,
> In light inaccessible hid from our eyes.

The Christian faith claims that, although God remains invisible, He did not leave Himself inaccessible, but communicated to us His essential nature and purpose in a human being, Jesus. The essential nature and purpose of God could be communicated in a human life because in all human beings there is a likeness to God, though distorted by choices and experiences. In Jesus there was a man who reflected the essential nature and purpose of God through God's love of Him and His love of God. His experience and His choices did not distort the likeness of God, but rather revealed more and more of God in Him. In His life, His Passion and His Cross, He showed that God is love. Such love is not defeated by death – nor was He. For those who come to believe that Jesus is God made known, then love becomes the goal of life. It is amazing that the word "love" has survived its constant debasement. I think it is because even the most pathetic, stained and comical expressions of our love are signs of the divine hunger for love that we all feel.

It is not easy to define love. We may be able to describe what it looks like, or know what it feels like, but it is difficult to say what it is. It is not just wanting the best for another person, because in wanting that, we are wanting something important for ourselves. It is not only God's love for us because we have the capacity, and He wants us to love Him. It is not just a spiritual love because we are physical beings and our bodies can be loving. It is not just a physical love, either, because it can be profound without any physical expression. It is not just one to one, or a family matter, but, in social justice, it is a matter for whole communities and nations.

For the Christian it is Christ who defines the love of God. This demonstration and definition are not only through the life and teaching of Jesus, but also through the Spirit of Christ in every age. In our midlife, we are often looking for our essential nature and purpose, and the love we see in Christ can be what we are looking for – "the Way, the Truth and the Life". Setting out on "the second half", with faith in the God and Father of our Lord Jesus Christ, is not the same as setting out without it. I am going to describe what seem to me to be the most important differences.

"Thy will be done"

Jesus instructed His followers to pray "Thy will be done". The words are the sharpest reminders to us that we are here for God's purpose. Even for Jesus, it was a struggle to do God's will. His life began in the most vulnerable setting. When He tried to work out what He should be and do, He spent time in the desert and was subjected to great temptations. Should He take worldly power? Should He prove who He was by performing miracles? He was even tempted to put evil in the place of God. This was not a foregone conclusion – they were real temptations. Through His life, He faced many moments of defeat, of amazement at the ingratitude, intolerance and hypocrisy of people. Once, in an expression of intense loneliness, He said:

> Foxes have their holes, the birds their roosts; but the Son of Man has nowhere to lay his head.
>
> Matthew 8:20

Before facing His final journey to face death, "His heart was ready to break with grief" and He asked God to give Him another destiny – but in it all, day by day, and at the end, He found a strong enough love of God to say "not my will, but thine be done".

This picture of the man struggling to do God's will does not fit into much of the contemporary analysis. I opened a book which claims to be the record-breaking, Number One bestseller about us and our personality, and on its first page it has a quote from Walt Whitman:

> The whole theory of the Universe is directed unerringly on one individual – namely to You.
>
> Dr Wayne W. Dyer, *Your Erroneous Zones*

His theme is to persuade us that we are not nearly as helpless as we think, that we have the ability to control ourselves and achieve our own happiness. Guilt, the fear of failure, worry, can all be banished by positive thinking, positive choosing and positive action. This is bracing stuff. It's down to me. I have only myself and my own values to answer to. There is an element of healthy teasing in all this, but I use the example because I believe it represents the base line of much popularized psychology. If we have only ourselves and our own values to answer to, then we shall certainly arrive at a rather different self than someone who prays to God "Thy will be done". In practice, the love of God encourages much of the life affirmation, the self-respect and the freedom from anxiety which are prescribed for the contemporary seeker after personality, but the "self" does not fill the centre of the stage, nor provide the only worthwhile values. It is a journey in love and, as in all such journeys, there is another's will to be considered.

It may be argued that at least we know, or often know, what we want, whereas we can't be at all sure what God wants. But the mystery of others is one of life's enduring excitements, and the mystery of God is one of the most beautiful mind and heart openers. To search for His will is like a man who gave up everything to search for a priceless treasure. It is a reason why we pray, why we read the Bible, why we worship, why we talk with people who have found some clues. These are the ways our minds can meet with the mind of God. By loving, and listening and learning, failing and starting again, we discover what He wants us to be and to do. It is not often that we receive such detailed instructions – though sometimes it is unnerving how clear they are – but rather His will is usually something which in the process of life we come to know and understand. There is the vast range of human experience of God to search in as well as our own.

Jesus approved this summary of God's law:

Love the Lord your God with all your heart, with all your
soul, with all your strength, and with all your mind; and
your neighbour as yourself.

Luke 10:27

"That is the right answer . . . do that and you will live", said
Jesus.

We are not the centre of the universe, however much we
like to think we are. It seems odd to us that people once
believed that the sun rotated around the earth. When you
begin to think seriously about what God wants your life to be,
it feels as odd to think that at one time you believed
everything rotated around you. To start thinking about God
and to start saying and trying to mean, and then trying to live
"Thy will be done", is in itself a positive crisis.

The "will of God" is a pretty sizeable demand to take on
board. It could threaten to overwhelm us and sink us in a
sense of guilt and inadequacy, and there has been a great
volume of justified criticism against this damaging distortion
of religion. It is important to remember that God's will is to
love us, and love casts out fear. This was the discovery that St
Paul made through his own life crisis.

He was a zealous disciple of pharisaic religion. We learn
that he lived as a passionate keeper of the law. His view of
Judaism seems to have lacked its humour and down-to-earth
realism. In terms of the definition I quoted earlier, he was
dominated by "the Parent" in him, pursued by his sense of
obligation. He was striving for perfection – to obey the whole
law, and in his moral striving was fierce against any who
threatened his value system. He was the archetype of the
person dominated by the "oughts" in his life, and doing
severe damage to himself and to others. All this came to
breakdown point. Because he believed the demands of God's
righteousness were so fierce, in his heart he knew they were
impossible. Then, as he struggled with God, he saw the light
of Christ, and grace poured in. He was at last free of the
harassing "parent" and found in Christ's love for him a new
life. The law had taught him what was right and wrong, and

yet it trapped him because he knew he could not keep it:

> The commandment which should have led to life proved in my experience to lead to death.
>
> Romans 7:10

In this way he became a divided self:

> I do not even acknowledge my own actions as mine, for what I do is not what I want to do, but what I detest . . . The good which I want to do, I fail to do; but what I do is the wrong which is against my will.
>
> Romans 7:15,19

This predicament, which is familiar as a personal experience to most of us (not just to those who are trying to do the will of God), led him to describe human nature as a tussle between the will of God and his own will.

> In my inmost self I delight in the law of God, but I perceive that there is in my bodily members a different law, fighting against the law that my reason approves.
>
> Romans 7:22–23

In his encounter with Christ, he learnt that God loved him and that this love was the basis of the good life. The will of God is not a trap, or a whip, or a warder, it is the way that His love directs us, and keeping it will lead us to the self we are seeking. A Jewish writer describing the "Torah" (the Law) as the way to embrace life wisely and well, said:

> The man who does these things will know security, for his way of life is ordered by the will and purpose of the Lord of man's history . . . Israel rejoices in the gift of the Torah. It is no burden to be borne with resignation, but a divine vade mecum to direct her on her course through life.
>
> *The Way of Israel*, p.115

Or, as the psalmist put it:

> The law of the Lord is perfect and revives the soul.
>
> Psalm 19:7

Whether the will of God for us is known through the teachings or prayer or the conscience, it is a way of love, for our fulfilment, not for our condemnation. Jesus' special word for God, ABBA, conveys the intimate way a child speaks to its loving father. A loving father does not set his children impossible tasks. All of us have many tapes in our experience first "recorded" by our own father. For some people, they are bad and damaging experiences, for others they stand for positive, loving and secure feelings. For Jesus, the word most truly expressed His love for God, and God's love for Him. For if there is a God, then however "adult" we are in this world, we shall find it is no offence to our very self to recognize our dependence.

> For all who are moved by the Spirit of God are sons of God. The Spirit you have received is not a spirit of slavery leading you back into a life of fear, but a Spirit that makes us sons, enabling us to cry "Abba! Father!"
>
> Romans 8:14–15

That cry ABBA is the cry of the child in us, it is a good and beautiful longing for the love of God, the key which unlocks inside us the gate of our own dreaded egocentricity. Our Father in Heaven . . . Thy will be done.

Self-acceptance – Self-giving – Self-realization

As I have said in an earlier chapter, Jesus restored to people who had a low self-image their sense of their own value. Whilst He challenged and accused the self-righteous and the self-satisfied, He brought a new assurance to those who felt unworthy, inadequate or guilty. Whether it was a leper, a

Samaritan, a tax gatherer or a prostitute, His love restored their sense of dignity. "Love to the loveless shown that they might lovely be." His word to the adulteress – "neither do I condemn thee" – was His essential acceptance of her before He said the hard word requiring change, "Go and sin no more!" No doubt the woman condemned herself and was ashamed to be so exposed, but Jesus' love was able to reach her shame and heal it. St Paul took up the theme of Christ's acceptance of us when he said:

> Whilst we were yet sinners, Christ died for us.
>
> Romans 5:8

For many Christians, the discovery that we are loved by God right to our inmost self is the beginning of self-acceptance and a proper self-love. If I am loved by God, when He knows everything about me, then I must be lovable.

For this important reason, Christian teachers and counsellors have been able to endorse the encouraging and accepting message to be found in psychology. Many people fight for years against their true selves, persistently doing themselves down, lacking in confidence and self-respect. It is a release to learn through the acceptance of others that we are lovable and worthwhile.

The next psychological stage in this self-discovery is the instruction which has become a cliché – "Be yourself". "Don't feel that you need others' approval all the time, don't get trapped by their demands and expectations, but be yourself." Again, this contains an important truth, challenging us to use our new-found self-respect and not submit to the bullying tactics of others, and certainly not bury ourselves and our talents. But we soon realize that it is unrealistic – perhaps impossible – to be ourselves. We immediately encounter the people around us, our families, our friends, our dependants, who presumably also deserve the chance to be themselves. We are free, but the scope of our own freedom will depend upon how that freedom affects others.

A release of the inner self is an essential stage on the road to freedom, but the freedom itself has to be expressed in the love of others. Gail Sheehy says:

> The most important words in midlife are "Let go". Let it happen to you. Let it happen to your partner. Let the feelings. Let the changes.
>
> *Passages*, p.364

But on this basis, the affairs, the separations, the divorces, the broken families, the throwing away of hard-won victories, could all be justified. What if your partner does not want it to happen? What if your children are terrified by the rows and the turmoil? What if the people you work with depend upon you, and their dependants depend upon them? Our own agenda is only one of the many agendas in which we are involved. We may have a fantasy that everything can work out as we would like it, and then realize that what is fantasy to us is a nightmare for everyone else.

I have no easy solution to this conflict between self-sacrifice and self-realization. It goes right to the heart of us. I believe there is a way of "being oneself" which is drawn from a vision of what that self can and should be. The vision we have of what we could be may be far less than the vision God may have for us. If you want to love the people who love and depend upon you, and do not want to damage and hurt them, then that is a good part of you. It may be the best and most important part. It may not feel like that. There may appear to be many attractive alternatives. But if you decide to stick, there will almost certainly be a whole range of ways in which your present life can be improved, the relationships enriched and some fulfilment found. Accept and receive your feelings, they are an expression of the essential you, but at the same time recognize that the essential you is a loving father, mother, brother, son, daughter, partner etc., etc., and you will not be able easily to put them all second to your own fulfilment.

We have to be ourselves, yet the followers of Jesus are

following a "man for others". Our fulfilment is not found in self-assertion, but in self-giving. It is impossible to find compromise between the two approaches. We cannot subscribe to "Let go. Let it happen to you . . . " if it is in conflict with the command to be servants of one another – to love our neighbour (including our partner!) as ourselves. The hard saying of Jesus remains:

> Whoever cares for his own safety is lost; but if a man will let himself be lost for my sake and for the Gospel, that man is safe.
>
> Mark 8:35

The process in Christian terms seems to be this. We begin with the self-affirmation that we are valued and loved by God. We need have no fear of allowing our feelings, our inner thoughts, our hidden selves into the conscious self – where we accept and offer that self to God. In the love of God, the self we inwardly hope to be can begin to grow, and may lead us to the mature self which God believes we can be. There is a proper self-love, there is a proper self-assertion, but they are relative to the rights to self-realization of those our decisions affect. We have Christ's promise that we can have life in all its abundance. If the way of love in our relationships and circumstances fits our own desires, we may rejoice in it – if it does not, we may have to carry for years the personal pain of taking such a course. That suffering can be part of the love which redeems the world.

The Reality of Evil

It has interested me to observe that in so many contemporary analyses of the human personality there is a reluctance to talk about wickedness. The prevailing view seems to be that if only people had well-adjusted parents, or could unravel the complexity of their life, or did not experience tragedy, or could accept themselves, then somehow wholesome, good, loving human beings would emerge. This is based on the assumption that if we are treated aright and understand ourselves, we shall be good. I have sympathy with this trend, and indeed it is often the right and helpful corrective when we accuse ourselves too much. But it simply will not do as a working hypothesis for mankind. In our century we have seen positive evil in full cry, and the optimism of liberal humanism is in ruins. It neither does justice to the facts of my own inward self, nor can I see it doing justice to the great world outside. The idea that goodness is the inevitable result of well-being is unrealistic, as those who live in splendid surroundings, have had excellent education, enjoy good health and great opportunities constantly demonstrate.

Jesus' picture of the human personality seems much more realistic, and therefore in the end more hopeful. The midlife search is not just a question of psychological readjustment, it is also another stage in the lifelong battle between good and evil. Jesus' picture of this battle involved a war between the God of love, whom He called Father, and the spirit of the Evil One, whom He called by various names – Satan, Beelzebub, the Tempter or the Accuser. In Hebrew, "Satan" means the "adversary", and Satan appears as the accuser of men in the heavenly court (Job 1:6ff). Beelzebub means "The Lord of the Fly" and was another name for the chief spirit of evil. This mythological framework is difficult for us to accept, but we can recognize the reality of evil it was used to describe. All through the gospels, the battle is joined. Jesus' own conflict in the wilderness tempted Him to worship the evil one, and take to Himself the power he possessed to conquer the world. Later, when Jesus said to His disciples that He was going to suffer, Peter rebuked Him, but Jesus responded fiercely:

> Away with you, Satan; you are a stumbling block to me. You think as men think, not as God thinks.
>
> Mark 8:33

Satan was seen as enticing people away from the will of God, fracturing their personality and testing their determination to live out love's demands. Part of the impact of Jesus and His disciples in their time was the power they had to drive out the evil spirits from the sick and the possessed. Judas' defection to the authorities was described in St Luke by the words "Satan entered him" (Luke 23:3). In John's Gospel, Jesus speaks of the battle against the powers of darkness. Darkness in the Old and New Testaments symbolized the whole threat of destruction – the empire of fear and violence and, in the end, non-being. Jesus' coming brings the judgement on the power of darkness:

> Now is the hour of judgement for this world; now shall the Prince of this world be driven out.
>
> John 12:31

The advocate i.e. the spirit who defends us against the evil accuser, will

> show that the Prince of this world stands condemned.
>
> John 16:11

The coming of Christ was the beginning of the victory of light over darkness. This battle reached to the heart of every man.

> All that came to be was alive with his life, and that life was the light of men. The light shines on in the dark, and the darkness has never mastered it . . . The real light which enlightens every man was even then coming into the world.
>
> John 1:4–5,9

The battle within each of us between good and evil was being fought in Christ. Although expressed in an archaic way, as seen and understood by people of the first century AD, the reality it describes is much the same as ours. We live in a world where evil is still unchecked, in spite of all our new technology and knowledge. The picture of life as a conflict between good and evil is important for us as individuals and as a race. The mythology which Jesus accepted was as much a part of His way of looking at life and God as our myths are part of us. In a time of cheap and transient myths, it may be important for us to have a new humility towards the world view of the Son of Man.

We do not have to travel far to explore the reality of evil, because it can and should be studied in the battlefield of our own mind. If we find it there, we can be sure that in the affairs of society, in the great affairs of the nations, it will be rampant. I am convinced that some of the bad things I have done and imagined are not just the result of being hard-done-by. The hurts which I have received have seemed to make me more ready to hurt others, but it is difficult to escape the idea that some of my worst thoughts and actions arrive in my mind under their own power. The conversation in my mind suggests that there is a voice or an impulse which offers me the bad alternative. I can then have all sorts of arguments with another voice or set of impulses which try to prevent me. Is this just the "computerized" response based on my past experience? Am I programmed to respond in this way by the "parent" in me, or by the hurt I have suffered in the past? It is puzzling, if that is the case, that I can analyse and explain it to myself, point out all the possible damage it will do, yet at the same time do it. The sources of evil in myself could be in part the result of stored resentment and anger, and in part the replay of the strongest and most passionate experiences on my own tape, in part the fearful reaction to the threatened loss of love. Yet those descriptions do not seem to me to describe adequately the independence of the evil within me. I am led to believe that the impulse, the energy and the will behind the evil I have done are not just a facet of my past experience, but rather a reality against which I have to struggle.

It is amazing how the energy and ammunition of evil is primed and ready to spring into action. It is so hard for the good in me to thrive. It is as though there is a computer operator deliberately selecting the difficult memories or playing the most depressing tapes. We do have considerable control over which tapes we play. We can, to some extent, choose to listen or to reject them. We are sometimes hooked on the damaging and difficult ones. But that does not seem a sufficient explanation, and I am left with the question, "Is this computer operator the hidden function of my own self, or is there some transcendent source?" Those of us who believe in God, believe that God can be positively involved in our thinking and feeling. We also believe that the Spirit of God can enter our consciousness. It is not difficult to believe that there is an accuser, a tempter, a stimulus of the evil. André Gide quotes *The Deliverance of Mark Rutherford*, volume 2, p.113:

> The shallowest of mortals is able now to laugh at the notion of a personal devil. No doubt there is no such thing existent; but the horror at evil which could find no other expression than in the creation of a devil is no subject for laughter, and if it do not in some shape or other survive, the race itself will not survive. No religion, so far as I know, has dwelt like Christianity with such profound earnestness on the bisection of man – on the distinction within him, vital to the very last degree, between the higher and the lower, heaven and hell. What utter folly is it because of an antique vesture to condemn as effete what the vesture clothes! Its doctrine and its sacred story are fixtures in concrete form of precious thoughts purchased by blood and tears.

Journals 1889–1949, p.241

Jesus believed there was the evil one – the evil side – the prince of darkness. It emerged through the mind and heart of man, both individually and corporately, and it had to be fought. The mythology was a way of describing this evil. Nothing could be more dangerous than to under-estimate the reality of evil – except possibly to credit it with too much power. Whether this tendency to do wrong comes from within myself or within the human race, its reality is vivid and challenges us to fight the good fight. We have the drama of the struggle. If the darkness and shadow are not part of the portrait, the human being is drawn in pale pastel and bears little resemblance to the sharply defined conflict of our experience. The battle within us is not just an unravelling of the self and the maturity of the "adult" who is there in waiting, because when the adult emerges he will still have the battle against evil. The more maturity, the deeper the perceptions, the higher the virtue – the stronger will be the sensitivity to evil and the ensuing battle.

The Golden Calf

In midlife we face in sharpest form the question about where and how we invest our lives. We can be tempted into finding our comfort in false gods. Having lived through our first thirty-five to forty years flat out, according to our own impetus and purpose, suddenly we can be faced with anxiety and doubt in the onset of middle age. What do we now see as worthy of adoration? What is it in our life which matters most to us? The new patio, the new car, the next promotion, the next woman, the rise in share prices, our microwave oven, our desire to be always right, our desire to win, our desire for popularity, our desire to get away from it all? The ancient story of Israel presents a contemporary choice, a challenge to Christian and Jew, and, I believe, to all God's children. We, like them, are called to freedom, but so often turn back from its discomfort into the devil we know. We struggle to choose life, but stumble over and over again into what is deadly for us.

All our individual identity crises pale in comparison with the identity crisis of the Chosen People. The rescue from slavery, the journey in the wilderness and the conquest of the promised land became for Israel the demonstration of God's favour. Wherever they have experienced persecution, oppression, pogroms and holocaust, they have drawn on this faith.

But although the Old Testament speaks of them as the Chosen People, this privilege does not guarantee their holiness. They vacillate in the wilderness between faithful obedience to God and disobedience and idolatry. How quickly they had forgotten the discomfort of slavery. They rebuked Moses for bringing them into a costly freedom:

> If only we had died at the Lord's hand in Egypt, where we sat round the fleshpots and had plenty of bread to eat! But you have brought us out into this wilderness to let this whole assembly starve to death.
>
> Exodus 16:3

Freedom is a costly business. When faced with the demands and tests of a free people, Israel, like the rest of us, was tempted to idolatry. They could not bear the uncertainty of freedom, and they said to Aaron:

> Come, make us gods to go ahead of us. As for this fellow Moses who brought us up from Egypt, we do not know what has become of him.
>
> Exodus 32:1

Whatever Aaron's motives, he invited them to bring all their gold. They built a god in the image of a bull-calf, bowed down before it, sacrificed to it and said:

> These are your gods, O Israel, that brought you up from Egypt.
>
> Exodus 32:4

The worship of the golden calf immediately led the people into moral chaos, and Moses, returning from the mountain with the commandments of God, found them engaged in an orgy. In his fury, he shattered the stone tablets – Israel had been offered life and they had chosen death. The Lord had rescued them from slavery, had brought them to freedom and had given them the Torah – the way to live – and at the first test they had failed.

This is the continuing story of Israel in the Old Testament – when they turn to the Lord their God and obey His commandments, a genuine future opens up for them, but when they turn to idols and allow injustice to prosper in the land, then they experience despair. The Lord makes specific demands of His people:

> to loose the fetters of injustice . . . and set free those who have been crushed . . . sharing your food with the hungry, taking the homeless poor into your house, clothing the naked when you meet them and never evading a duty to your kinsfolk.
>
> Isaiah 58:6–7

There was a clear vision of what was expected of the people of God. But they turned their backs on goodness and obedience, and chose the shining gods of gold, power and sensuality.

Jesus was a child of the tradition, and taught that we become the product of what we worship. What we value most highly in life makes us the sort of people we are – "Where your treasure is – there will your heart be also." He also showed that the investment of ourselves in material riches led to emptiness of soul.

> Then he said to the people, "Beware! Be on your guard against greed of every kind, for even when a man has more than enough, his wealth does not give him life." And he told them this parable: "There was a rich man whose land yielded heavy crops. He debated with himself: 'What am I to do? I have not the space to store my produce . . . I will pull down my store-houses and build them bigger. I will collect in them all my corn and other goods, and then say to myself, "Man, you have plenty of good things laid by, enough for many years: take life easy, eat, drink and enjoy yourself." ' But God said to him, 'You fool, this very night you must surrender your life; you have made your money – who will get it now?' That is how it is with the man who amasses wealth for himself and remains a pauper in the sight of God."
>
> Luke 12:15–21

Jesus knew that man is often fooled by outward security and comfort into thinking it will bring him happiness and love, and that he positively goes on choosing what is bad for him. This remains the source of so much human tragedy. The drug addict, the alcoholic, the compulsive gambler, choose what leads to their misery and even death, because of an illusion of relief or happiness. The unrestrained pursuit of money often leads to a corresponding loss of spontaneity, generosity, faith, warmth of affection, humility and happiness. It remains a fundamental and accurate statement about us all, that alongside the good and loving things we do, we also choose what is bad for us, and hurtful for those around us. Jesus related this choice to the way we look out on life, the way we react to what we see. That "look" is the frontline of the personality.

> The lamp of your body is the eye. When your eyes are sound, you have light for your whole body, but when the eyes are bad, you are in darkness.
>
> Luke 11:34

We are motivated by the way we look at people and things around us, and the way in which our inner self tackles what we see.

Deciding how to invest our lives, setting a value on what we see, choosing our priorities, is not just a question of our heart's desire. The second half of our life will see the harvest of our choices. If we stick at the job which we know degrades us or keeps us in a rut, then after another twenty years of such "security" we may well be boring or embittered. If we settle into an impoverished marriage relationship because improvement requires courage, we shall reap loneliness and resentment in old age. If our work means everything to us, we shall have to face losing our major personal source of fulfilment. If we spend all our energy building and equipping a luxury home for ourselves, what will we have left if we go broke, or lose a child, or have a heart attack?

We make our choices and they make us.

Forgiveness and Grace

The other main difference between Jesus' teaching about human nature and the secular maps of personality relates to the power of forgiveness as the great healing agent. I have already talked about the importance of forgiveness in marriage, but it is obviously true of all our relationships. When faced with the burden and threat of all the recorded tapes in our personality which we replay so consistently, it is not difficult to see how important is the power to change them, not only by the forgiveness of God, but also by the forgiveness we offer each other. "Forgive us our sins as we forgive those who sin against us" is one of our central prayers. When we forgive each other and we can accept it, healing takes place. When God forgives us and we accept it, then that is a great source of new hope in a person's life.

> Wash away all my guilt
> and cleanse me from my sin.
> For well I know my misdeeds,
> and my sin confronts me all the day long.
>
> Take hyssop and sprinkle me, that I may be clean;
> wash me, that I may become whiter than snow.
>
> Psalm 51:2–3,7

The result of this forgiveness is that the slate is wiped clean – the tape, if not erased, is disarmed, and the restored and healed person can experience the hope and happiness of a new beginning.

That sounds easier than it is. Our habitual actions and attitudes die hard. All the choices we have made, all the things that people have done to us, and all the hurt we have done to others, become part of us. It is not helpful when

185

people try to persuade us that something we know to have
been wrong was not really wrong at all. Sometimes we need a
straightforward judgement, to restore our sense of self-
respect. Shame can be highly misleading and may just be a
programmed response, but there are times when it is the
necessary, right, healthy, adult reaction to something we
have done. We need to find a way of facing it and then putting
it behind us and not allowing ourselves to play its tape over
and over again. If God's forgiveness is offered, then it is a lack
of trust if we can't believe it and accept it. The psalmist
reminds us of the immense range and power of God's
forgiveness:

> The Lord is compassionate and gracious,
> long-suffering and for ever constant;
> he will not always be the accuser
> or nurse his anger for all time.
> He has not treated us as our sins deserve
> or requited us for our misdeeds.
> For as the heaven stands high above the earth,
> so his strong love stands high over all who fear him.
> Far as east is from west,
> so far has he put our offences away from us.
> As a father has compassion on his children,
> so has the Lord compassion on all who fear him.
>
> Psalm 103:8–13

This is a lovely belief and a wonderful assurance to have at the
heart of our lives. But the fact is, that even when we accept it
and we feel the burden lifted from us, we set out again and
allow ourselves to fail all over again. They call someone who
keeps on going back into prison a recidivist, because he finds
prison easier to cope with than the outside world. It is what
he's used to, and to change would require enormous effort
and courage to make and carry out his own decisions. We can
be like that about the actions which drag us down. We grow
addicted to them and almost prefer them to the pain of real
change. Forgiveness opens the prison door and allows us

back our freedom, and maybe even gives us enough enthusiasm to survive for a few days in the outside world, but only
real change of heart will prevent us from committing the same
offence again.

In the Old Testament, Ezekiel expresses the bleak opinion
that we are unable to change by our own will power. He says
there is something rebellious and deceitful in the heart of man
which constantly lures him away from God and what leads to
happiness. His inner self builds such a resistance against the
love of God, and so invests himself in the worldly ways, that
some new act of God is needed. Forgiveness is not enough,
because the people are so addicted to the ways of disobedience
that they have lost the ability to change. God's new initiative
will have to take place within the very personality of man.

> I will give them a different heart and put a new spirit in
> them; I will take the heart of stone out of their bodies and
> give them a heart of flesh. Then they will conform to my
> statutes and keep my laws.
>
> Ezekiel 11:19–20

Christians believe that this act of God was the gift of a new
spirit. If there is an accuser and a tempter in us, putting on the
old, disheartening, damaging tapes, there is also the Spirit of
God working with us to choose the good and loving way. Jesus
called this Spirit the Advocate. He defends us against our past
and opens up the real possibility of change. We still make the
choices and the decisions. We still have the power to go on
playing the old tapes, of going back into old habits, or
choosing slavery, but the good desire in us has a most
powerful ally. This loving, intimate strength comes from the
love of God through His Spirit, and we call it Grace. St Paul
wrote:

> The harvest of the Spirit is love, joy, peace, patience, kind-
> ness, goodness, fidelity, gentleness, and self-control.
> There is no law dealing with such as these . . . If the Spirit

is the source of life, let the Spirit also direct our course.

Galatians 5:22–25

The Grace of God gives us the power, through the Spirit, to choose love as the most excellent way.

10

The Way Ahead

It is difficult to hold together the insights of psychology, theology, theories of personal development and our experience. They tug this way and that, and can lead up theoretical cul-de-sacs, and sometimes it is hard to see how they relate to you and me.

In his book, Father Gerald O'Collins rejects the word "crisis" for the midlife experience. " 'Midlife crisis' sounds just a little too negative", he says.

> Of course, someone will always remind us that, after all, crises may turn out to be challenges to a false status quo and opportunities for future growth and true renewal. Nevertheless, no amount of coaxing will take away the negative and gloomy aura which clings to the word "crisis". One way or another, any crisis threatens to rip our life apart at the seams. It suggests primarily a menace.
>
> *The Second Journey*, p.16

The word crisis derives from the Greek *krisis* – a word which has a marvellous array of meanings, some of which are very applicable to the present theme. It is the title of a play by Sophocles about the Judgement of Paris – a man who, by his compulsive love of Helen, caused a war! It could mean "acting with judgement", i.e. evaluating the situation and coming to a wise judgement about the future. It can be the judgement of the court where we are put on trial. It can refer, in an illness, to the turning point for better or worse – the critical period. It can mean discernment, in the sense of understanding dreams and portents.

In the New Testament, it most often refers to the Day of Judgement, when each individual will be called to account for what they have been. It can refer to justice for the individual and the world:

> Alas for you, lawyers and Pharisees, hypocrites! You pay
> tithes of mint and dill and cumin; but you have overlooked
> the weightier demands of the Law, *justice*, mercy and
> good faith. It is these you should have practised, without
> neglecting the others.
>
> Matthew 23:23

Or right judgements, as in John 7:24:

> Do not judge superficially, but be just in your *judgements*.

Perhaps its strongest use is in Jesus' words:

> Now is the hour of *judgement* for this world; now shall the
> Prince of this world be driven out.
>
> John 12:31

– a passage which concentrates on the urgency of the present
moment, the call to a choice between a way of life and a way of
death. Jesus also describes the Spirit which He sent as One

> [who] when he comes, he will confute the world and show
> where wrong and right and *judgement* lie.
>
> John 16:8

"Midlife judgement" sounds even more threatening than
midlife crisis, but maybe there is a threat as well as a promise
in the time. The Spirit of God is experienced not only as the
encouragement and affirmation – "You're OK" – but also as
a critique which can challenge us to become a new self. The
encounter with God is the encounter with love. Love is an
enriching, nourishing experience, yet true love often
involves judgement, because it loves the person that can be,
as well as the person that is. This sharp edge is as strong and
good for us as the beautiful acceptance which love offers.
There is something tiresome about the person who can see no

faults in us – almost as tiresome (but not quite) as the person who can't see any good in us. The coach has his stopwatch and his eyes, and sometimes he will say "That's great", and at other times – out of his desire for the success of the athlete – he will say "That's not good enough". He may even come to the point when he says, "If you go on eating and drinking at the present level, there is nothing I can do to help – you'll never make an athlete."

I think that the word "crisis" is helpful when understood as a decisive turning point. If you are a non-believer in God, then midlife is such a turning point when you can take steps towards the person you think you should be, according to your own value system. If you believe in God or are looking, then it is a turning point when particular issues in your life come to a head, and it is necessary for you to think and pray about how it is between you and God, as reflected in the way you lead your life, and, from that reflection – that evaluation – should follow new decisions and actions. What we discover in this critical time will almost certainly in some ways affirm, encourage, strengthen what we have been up to this point, show us what are the claims of a proper self-love, and in other ways bring sharply before us the deterioration of our ideals, the development of our masks and the injustice of our relationships. If we do not face up to this "crisis", then it is possible that we shall drag our midlife unhappiness, resentment, apathy, through with us into middle age, which will be to miss out on an intensely rich time of life, and will certainly carry forward into old age disheartening problems of our personality, which could have been resolved. Many of the problems in middle age, and certainly in old age, relate to people's refusal to accept the rhythm and pace of their lives. It was Jung who said:

The very frequent neurotic disturbances of adult years have this then in common, that they betray the attempt to carry the psychic dispositions of youth beyond the threshold of the so-called years of discretion.
Modern Man in Search of a Soul, p.121

This process goes on. For instance, the refusal to retire and put down the busyness and authority of middle age is sometimes a sign that at midlife (35 to 45 plus) there was no real attempt to discover a self which was not solely dependent on them.

In *As You Like It*, what is so melancholy about Jaques is the passivity with which the stages of life have to be endured. It is as though there is nothing the person can do to escape the tedious sameness of the journey, no steps to be taken to adopt positive attitudes at each stage of life. Men and women are merely actors in a play that's already written:

> . . . And then the lover,
> Sighing like furnace, with a woeful ballad
> Made to his mistress' eyebrows. Then a soldier,
> Full of strange oaths, and bearded like the pard,
> Jealous in honour, sudden and quick in quarrel,
> Seeking the bubble reputation
> Even in the cannon's mouth. And then the justice,
> In fair round belly with good capon lin'd,
> With eyes severe and beard of formal cut,
> Full of wise saws and modern instances;
> And so he plays his part.
>
> *As You Like It*, Act 2, Scene 7

There is something puppet-like about those players – however much they may seem to express their own freedom. We should look for a greater individuality than that. Whilst we must play out the physical drama, we can develop and exercise the soul which is our eternal self in love with God. As Gerald O'Collins says, we can

> become participants in, rather than victims of, what we experience.
>
> *The Second Journey*, p.66

Gail Sheehy says:

> The courage to take new steps allows us to let go of each
> stage with its satisfactions and to find the fresh responses
> that will release the richness of the next.
>
> *Passages*, p.514

There are "passages" to be negotiated and there are predictable crises of adult life.

You would think that with all the Church's rites of
passage, there would be a midlife rite to see us into middle
age. I don't think I'd better suggest one – it would not get
approval. I shall content myself with trying to say, as simply
and practically as I can, what conclusions I have reached
about this turning of the tide.

1. *Taking Stock*

Most of us have to take stock in midlife. Whether our crisis is
the result of the death of a loved partner, or the breaking of
our marriage, or the final outburst against the way things are,
or just a slow process as we accumulate the idea that
something, someone has to give. The sort of questions we
ought to face include: What sort of person have we become?
Where is life leading us? What are our relationships like?
What do we believe? What do we care about? What are we
hiding? What are our gifts, and are we using them? What are
our dreams, and are they just fantasies or could we take steps
to make them reality? What really bugs us, and what gives us
hope and strength? (Our strongest feelings are often the most
revealing material evidence of how it is with us.) What are
our ambitions and how realistic are they? What is the quality
of our family and personal life? Does our philosophy of life
carry the weight of our experience till now, and the future we
see ahead? Which are the repeated patterns in our lives which
increase our sense of being a worthwhile person, and which
decrease that self-respect? How are we going to change?

In this process of evaluation, it may be helpful to talk with someone else – but someone who loves us enough to give a judgement as well as comfort. If we are not truthful to ourselves, as far as we can see the truth, the process is a waste of time. It cannot just concern ourselves in isolation, because there are the lives of the people we directly and intimately affect. If we are married, we have to work out the contract which best expresses our partnership and our individuality. We also have to work out our relationships with our parents and our children, accept their season as well as our own and sort out the implications that their happiness and fulfilment have for us, and vice versa.

Although this can be a painful process, we do have a say in what sort of crisis it is – a turning point for the better or the worse.

The process will almost certainly muddy the water in our mental reservoir. If we search to understand how we have come to where we are, it will involve an assessment and attempt to understand what our parents made us, how our most powerful experiences and relationships have affected us, and what we have made of ourselves. This can be disturbing and confusing, as well as liberating and exciting. It can lead to momentary feelings of resentment, but it can resolve tensions we have never previously understood, create a sense of forgiveness and greater charity, and bring a sense of self-acceptance and a feeling of being "at home" in ourselves. It may well be that this self-reassessment will help us realize that changes have got to be made – relationships terminated or deepened, new recreation explored, new habits made and old habits broken. This radical reappraisal can offer us a new beginning, and it is a comfort to think that if the crisis had not happened, we might have slowly sunk into the rut of habitual personal lethargy which accepts the status quo as inevitable. One of the precious and wonderful things about God is that, because His mystery is inexhaustible, there is always new life waiting for us – "with God, breakdown can become breakthrough". With God these things are possible – with man they seem impossible. We might well be able to re-evaluate ourselves, begin to understand the past and feel ready to contemplate change in the future, but our nearest and dearest, our colleagues, our friends who provide the human context in which these changes have to take place, may strongly resist the new vision. They may prefer the way things are and have us as the old slippers they are used to. If they can be involved in the reappraisal and see its benefits, not only for us but for them, and if our liberation does not look like slavery to them, it may well be that they will come to welcome and share in its excitement. It is no good "bullying" or "hectoring" them to change at the same time and in the same ways. The "taking stock" may for some people lead to the realization that others are not going to change, and this will result in difficult and costly decisions. There is so much that can be done before such a failure, to discover reconciliation and a new start.

If there are destructive patterns in ourselves, we have to find out why they happened, and sometimes that may require expert help, or at least an objective listening ear. Then in the forgiveness of God we have to tackle them, by monitoring our efforts, by changing the situation, by sharing the tension, by finding suitable escape valves. The old tapes play on and we have to find the will not to choose to play them over and over again, never to lose hope, and to fill the empty spaces with new creative initiatives. Taking stock is the essential analysis of our midlife self in its relationship to others and to God, with a view to constructive change.

2. Pursue the Meaning

A friend of mine set himself the task of making a fortune by the time he was thirty-five. Brought up "tough" in East London, he threw himself totally into this goal. People used to say to him, "You'll have a heart attack." His reply was, "I'll laugh all the way to the crem!" Another man had a vision for his daughter – he believed she was going to be academically brilliant. He loved that image of her, and she desperately tried to fulfil his expectations. Both dreams fell in ruins. She was a lovely, kind, generous person, who became ashamed of her real gifts. A husband and wife set their sights on moving out to Essex. They both worked very hard to achieve it. They bought their house on a mortgage. They got there, and after six months were separated. A man gave himself heart and soul to his political party's manifesto. He lost sight of himself in selling it to others. A policeman was ambitious and he was reaching the top when his wife died. There was nothing left. A woman battled her way to the top of her profession and, too late, desperately wanted to suckle the baby she never had. A pop star grew accustomed to adoration, woke up to the fact that it had all come to an end, and he had no idea who he was or what was his purpose in life. A man reached the age of forty a tired, lonely sexual athlete.

All these are real people who have tackled life without finding their meaning. They chose and pursued objectives which flattered to deceive. I believe it is the prevailing sickness of our society that so many of us take the meaning for granted. Listen to yourself talk – what is your purpose? Have you got a sense of direction, and is it a direction which will give a meaning to the second half of your life? I have attempted to show how important Jung's insight is about having a mythology. In the golf club, the pub, on the beach at Ibiza, at the cocktail party, in the central lobby of the House of Commons, in the boardroom, in the canteen, in the Parochial Church Council, in bed, watching the telly – who are we? As we sit in the underground reading the half-truths in the press, walk in procession round a cathedral, decorate a room . . . again, what's it all for? "Eat, drink and be merry, for tomorrow we die" – fifty-five out of every hundred people prefer it! "Make the world a better place to live in?" – ten out of every hundred believe that in theory, but would rather it didn't change our life-style. "Live in quiet, uncomplaining apathy" – the "don't knows" have it.

I am expressing my anger about this because so many of us appear to sell ourselves cheap and waste the great potential we have. So many of our lives are like those weddings where everything is beautifully arranged, the people are beautiful, the service is beautiful, but there is no inward purpose. We can put on a splendid affluent show, but we're not at all sure why we are getting married. Midlife is a time when the external gratification can be impressive, but the internal meaning has dried up. I hope you might not leave God out of your pursuit of meaning. God is the preserver of meaning. The world without God is at best a brave theatre of the absurd. The world with God is a place of hope and purpose, in which each of us has value and a destiny.

A middle-aged man went night after night to his local. Every night he drank a half, made it last, and returned home. Night after night. He was "potentially" an adoptive grandfather of a baby he had not met, potentially a man of prayer whose spirit would help him look for the value and potential in others, a man of humour and kindness. Through discovering God, he achieved that potential. Though he was seventy-eight when he died, crowds of people came and cried at his funeral. There is a sentimental movie starring James Stewart called *It's a Wonderful Life*. In a deep depression, the suicidal George is shown a vision of his home town as if he had never been born – for that's what he wished. The familiar faces of his friends, his clients, his family, his wife, were unable to recognize him because he had never lived. He never knew what he had done for them all – it only became clear when he saw them as they would have been without him. If he had not had his sense of purpose, and had not found a meaning which kept him going through all their failures and defeats, other faces than his would have been filled with misery to prove the point. There is a sacred purpose for us all. Midlife can be the time when we find it, or perhaps miss it for good. There are so many "counterfeit destinations", as Gerald O'Collins calls them. The way that leads to life is often narrow and hard – the way that leads to nothing is broad and easy.

In the Parsee faith, there is the teaching that just as we are about to die our soul appears before us. The light glows through it according to the way we have lived. Our individual soul is precious. It must pull its weight. If we allow a vacuum in our soul, it will attract the bad spirits. Many bad spirits in the crowd make a great evil. Solzhenitsyn described the greatest evil of our time in this way:

> The spirit of Munich is the dominant spirit of the twentieth century. In answer to Hitler, the civilized world quailed at the onslaught of snarling barbarism, suddenly revitalized; the civilized world found nothing with which to oppose it, save concessions and smiles. The spirit of Munich is an illness of the will-power of the well-to-do, it is the usual state of those who have surrendered to the lust for comfort at any price, have surrendered to materialism as the main aim of our life on earth.
>
> *One Word of Truth*

We may not opt out of deciding what is the main aim of our life on earth. To discern the meaning and pursue what we see saves us and far more.

3. *The Life We Receive*

There are contrasting dangers in the midlife situation – the sense of failure and inadequacy on the one hand, and incipient pompousness, self-satisfaction and self-righteousness on the other. Most of us vacillate between them, but some "specialize" in one or the other. The Christian Gospel has something significant to say to both. To the person who is permanently "sorry" and regards themselves as a failure, Christ offers assurance that he or she is loved by God, and that there is always the possibility of a new future, alongside a warning against wallowing in self-pity. God will meet us where we are, love us there and then help us to move on. This requires an honest offering of self to God so that He can work through us. "Just as I am without one plea – Lamb of God, I come."

For the self-satisfied, there is a judgement and a reminder of how small a unit we are, in the universe. We may be fooled by success or power into thinking that we are superior to others, and that what we have achieved is our justification. Yet by that attitude, we can most deny God and reduce others. It is easy to lose our sense of reverence. The Bible reminds us over and over again that our lives are given by God – our time, our talents, our possessions are on loan to us for our earthly pilgrimage. In the Hindu religion the twice-born goes through four stages (Ashramas) in the ideal life:

(i) "Let the young man study the Vedas in due order, without breaking celibacy." This is the stage of the bachelor.

(ii) "After studying the Vedas, let him dwell in the householder order." This is the time of home and family.

(iii) "When the householder sees wrinkles [on his face] and whiteness [in his hair] and the son of his son, let him retire to the forest."

(iv) "After passing the third portion of his life in the forest and becoming free of all attachment, let him wander [as an ascetic] during the fourth portion."

Religious Hinduism, p.116

When the third stage is reached, the disciple "retires to the forest" for a period of learning detachment, and then, when he has discovered this freedom, he lives as a wandering mendicant, without shelter, without fire.

I can't see these stages catching on in twentieth-century Britain, but I believe there is something of great importance in their spirit. It is in the learning that our life is received from God and that in the end it all has to be returned to God. It seems to me to be a significant difference between Western and Eastern religions. I am not talking about a sort of fatalism, nor am I speaking in praise of idleness. It is rather something more fundamental about reverence for life, reverence for others and reverence for God. The physical position which puts me most in touch with God is to sit still with my hands on my lap, palms upturned in a "receiving" frame of mind. At the Eucharist, we reach up our hands to receive the bread of life. In our prayers, like the rest of our lives, we tend to batter God with our words and our thoughts and our emotions, and yet one of the basic lessons we are having to learn is that His Spirit is *given* to us and we receive it; we cannot earn it, or make it, or wind ourselves up to be perfect enough to deserve it, we can only receive it. This strikes at the heart of so much of our status-seeking, our self-justification, our self-satisfaction. We may properly climb the mountain and rejoice with the effort and the achievement, but the mountain, the air, the ice, the snow, our limbs, our lungs, our eyes, our courage, are the gift of God. We may celebrate the microchip, but we are only drawing upon an intrinsic miracle of the universe. The athlete is thrilled to breast the tape – he does so by having a rightly tuned, God-given body. As new parents we may be proud of our baby, and concentrate our energy and skill in raising a new person, but our share in the creation is humblingly limited – especially the man! Even the woman, like Mary, has to wait patiently and carry the new life she has received.

We Western Christians are so often activist and busy in our religion. Our faith is full of what we are going to do for God – so full of doing, yet so wary of being and receiving.

And Mary said:
"Tell out, my soul, the greatness of the Lord,
rejoice, rejoice, my spirit, in God my saviour;
so tenderly has he looked upon his servant,
humble as she is.
For from this day forth,
all generations will count me blessed,
so wonderfully has he dealt with me,
the Lord, the Mighty One.
His name is Holy."

Luke 1:46–49

This humble receiving from God does not lead to indolence or passivity or inactivity, but leads to the whole life being given back to God, and what follows is the radical unsettling of the established human order.

"The arrogant of heart and mind he has put to rout,
he has brought down monarchs from their thrones,
but the humble have been lifted high.
The hungry he has satisfied with good things,
the rich sent empty away."

Luke 1:51b–53

Our prayer in part is to remind ourselves that we are receiving the love of God, not forcing it by our own efforts, not creating it by our anxiety, and not earning it by our goodness. Whether we need to be humbled or encouraged in midlife, a key is to discover what life God is giving us. Being open to His love has this wonderful way of exalting the humble and bringing down the arrogant in each of us. Wholeness might lie in bringing the strength of both into middle age at the time of our midlife crossroads. The promotion is not everything, the success is not all-important. However anxious we get we cannot grow half an inch, we cannot drive ourselves to be happy, we cannot drive ourselves to be born, we cannot make ourselves perfect, we cannot live two lives in one, we cannot insure ourselves against suffering – in all these things we depend upon the inbreathing of God.

Then the Lord God formed man from the dust of the ground and breathed into his nostrils the breath of life.

Genesis 2:7

This dependence is the fundamental attitude and starting place of the good life. So, if we are successful people, let's see it for what it is – see through it and retain a reverence for others. If we are a failure, trust in God, recognize through faith that He has a destiny for us. Dignity is within, conferred by the love of God.

4. *Generosity of Life-style*

The Jew is called by the Torah to live generously because of the generosity of God. There are in the psalter songs of praise where the author reminds himself again and again of the goodness and generosity of the Lord:

> It is good to give thanks to the Lord
> for his love endures for ever.

> Psalm 136:1

If every living creature understood what God had done, they would all sing praises to God for the miracle of life. "Let everything that has breath, praise the Lord." The response expected of the Jew and the Christian, and indeed the adherents of all the great religions, is to live generously in return. For instance, even with all the fear of the alien and the stranger in the Old Testament, the Lord expects the generous reaction of the people of Israel to the alien in their midst:

> The Lord secures justice for widows and orphans, and loves the alien who lives among you, giving him food and clothing. You too must love the alien, for you once lived as aliens in Egypt.

> Deuteronomy 10:18–19

There is an example of the commandment to live generously, because that is God's nature and because God has given so generously to us.

Jesus gave this instruction to His disciples:

> Heal the sick, raise the dead, cleanse lepers, cast out devils. You received without cost, give without charge.

> Matthew 10:8

Or as the Authorized Version has it: "Freely ye have received, freely give." The giving flows from the receiving. The Good Samaritan lived generously – not only in the gift of money, but in the courage and thoroughness of his care. The more we have received, the more we are expected to give. It is sad how that is often reversed in our society. In a drought in Namibia, I stayed in a bombed-out seminary, and we had running water. Our hosts had been living for years of drought with dried-up rivers and polluted water holes. The crops were poor, the cattle were skeletal – and yet we had running water. I hardly noticed. It wasn't until later that I learnt of the sacrifices that had been made to give us running water such as we are used to here, so that we should be comfortable. So often I have found in my ministry that people who have little will give whatever they have, whereas the well-off insure, protect, build up what they have and argue intensely over the slightest financial advantage.

When I speak of a generous life-style, I am not just talking about giving resources – though that is important and not just something for individual magnanimity, but a matter of government policy in a civilized society. Rather, I am talking about the way we use all the resources we have, whether we have lots of money or none. I am referring to hospitality, availability, compassion, encouragement, cheerfulness, forgiveness, tolerance, kindness, appreciation, patience, sensitivity and so on. Our meanness reduces us. A friend of mine tells the true story of his grandmother, who was poor:

She loved laughter, and cheerfulness, and the poor, and people of all kinds, even the most unlovable, above all she loved giving, whether of herself in loving, in understanding and in her own great tolerance, or of her few material possessions, though this was harder for her to achieve, because her children, well aware of their mother's propensity for giving everything away, locked the cupboard and kept the key with one or other of them. But such little local difficulties could not daunt my angelic grandmother – when a poor woman came to the house and asked her for a sari, it was the most natural thing for my grandmother (her cupboard being locked) simply to take off the one she was wearing and give it to her, thanking her all the while for taking it. The fact that it was her best sari, just given by my mother, did not worry her in the least. She was very sorry for having upset my (somewhat justifiably, I suppose) irritated mother, but she was totally unrepentant about the rightness of her action. "You see, darling," she said to me in a conspiratorial aside, pressing my hand, "Kitty doesn't understand – the poor woman needed a sari, and" – and this was said very triumphantly – "she liked my one so much."

Midlife often brings changes which mean we can have more love and resources available for others. It often has to be an outgoing time because of the needs of sons and fathers, daughters and mothers, but it can also be a time when we take responsibility in society, when we give support rather than demand it, when we can contribute skill and experience. The generous life-style is not meant to diminish space and privacy, but it certainly should release us from self-pity and prepare us for middle age as a positive caring and outgoing person. It should certainly be a time of making and developing friendships – both acquaintances, and also those close friends who give and receive the most excellent nourishment.

5. *Body and Soul*

It is no good pretending that our body and soul are totally different parts of us. All that we are and do in the body, we do in the soul. The soul is not detached from the physical aspects of life. Religion – especially certain forms of Christianity – has often had a disastrous influence upon the way people think of their bodies and their sexual feelings and experience.

It is said in some manuals advising people on their sexual relationships, that their own satisfaction is the key, and if existing relationships get in the way, then they should probably side-step them. We seem to be faced with a choice of the severity of the old rules, or a sort of selfishness which puts the priority on our own individual satisfaction, irrespective of the damage that such satisfaction may do to others.

There is no doubt that sexual dissatisfaction plays a major part in human unhappiness. Many people live in permanent, melancholy regret because of the "might have beens" and "if onlys" of their sexual lives. We may develop harmful patterns over long years, whether in existing sexual relationships or in fantasies. Habits of life become part of the person we are, and slowly erode our hope or desire to change. The dissatisfaction can build up to such a level that it becomes a source of bitterness against the world, or against the partner. A wife shouts at her husband, "You've stolen my life!" Or one partner finds satisfaction outside the marriage, and this adds a whole set of reactions associated with guilt.

Much is written about the lack of sexual satisfaction through the failure to achieve orgasm, or the secret anger at the feeling of rejection within the sexual relationship itself. The books and manuals can describe as many sorts of dissatisfaction as there are cases. It makes sense to try to tackle the causes of these dissatisfactions as honestly as possible, where necessary with professional advice, but it is highly misleading and damaging to suppose that everyone will find enduring, total sexual satisfaction. That is not the real world. Sexual satisfaction is only one priority in a person's life, and will often have to take second place in the face of longer-term commitments and responsibility for others.

It may well be that a person has to face a lifetime of sexual disqualification through handicap or injury – it may be that the person we love has limitations physically or emotionally which deprive us of satisfaction – it may well be that we are also limited, normal, affectionate, amateur joggers in the sex olympics. Almost all married couples have to face decisions at some time between the survival of their marriage, the love and respect they hold for their partner, and the opportunity for personal sexual satisfaction with someone else.

Living in the real world imposes limits on self-realization – and this is not just confined to sexuality. It might suit us to have a vast increase in pay, but this might put others out of a job. It might be nice to have diamonds, but we may have them by robbing a third-world country. It might be fun to drink at a party, but we are responsible the moment we get into the car to drive home because we may be a killer. In most spheres of our life, the person who attends to God should see that there have to be limitations. In the long run they enhance proper self-interest. We grow rich, but it does not satisfy us because we have oppressed others. We grow merry, but we are putting ourselves and others at risk. We win, but others lose. The point was beautifully expressed by St Paul:

> You, my friends, were called to be free men; only do not turn your freedom into licence for your lower nature, but be servants to one another in love. For the whole law can be summed up in a single commandment: "Love your neighbour as yourself." But if you go on fighting one another, tooth and nail, all you can expect is mutual destruction.

> Galatians 5:13–15

We have responsibility for each other – our fulfilment seems so much more important than the fulfilment of others, but so often the selfish pursuit will leave us all discontented. So sexual satisfaction is not a right, it is, for the Christian, only achievable within the proper self-realization of the other people who make up the network of our lives. Decisions have to be made, choices lived out, and that is the stuff of ordinary life. We may want to have a new partner, and at the same time want our first partner to be happy and the children to live in happiness and security, but that is probably not possible. We may want to grow in integrity and proper self-respect, and yet lead a double life, but that is a contradiction in terms. Sexual satisfaction has to be put in its place in life's ambitions, and we must recognize that love may demand that we love in a way far from the technicolour spectaculars, and much nearer to curlers, and children bursting into the room – it never happens like this in James Bond's world . . .

I do not want to under-estimate the fear of losing youth and potency. At several times in our lives, sexual drive and needs become so important that we can think of little else. As I have said, midlife has a lot in common with a second adolescence, and for a time again, sexual fulfilment can loom very large in our thoughts. If it has been very satisfying, we can fear to lose it; if it has been very frigid and unfulfilling, then we can fear that we may never experience the bliss which is part fact and part fantasy. Our faith can put this side of our lives sharply into perspective. It's important to us – yes – but it is only one part of life. Maybe the most fulfilled sexual athlete has left a large part of the rest of his life untapped and undeveloped. There is so much to do, to understand, to be interested in, to study, to enjoy, to contribute, to give, to fight for, that sexual satisfaction can fall back into a more realistic place in the priorities of midlife. It is as misguided to rush away from sexual intimacy into work, creative interests, service in society, as it is to undervalue them and believe that all satisfaction is for some reason based upon sexual fulfilment.

So love is the goal – a love which has as much mutual pleasure as can be drawn from our relationship, with the adult recognition of the limitations on most people's sex life, and the essential recognition that "my" satisfaction and self-realization are only one side of the self-realization and satisfaction of the other people involved in my network of relationships.

If we believe that God made us, then He gave us our bodies, and it is most certain that He had every intention that we should reproduce ourselves, and that we should find physical love and comfort in each other. Yet this side of our life is responsible for more hang-ups, more guilt, more accusations, more unhappiness, than almost any other. A psychiatrist rather sharply said that he knew in which particular part of the body he would locate "guilt". The wearers of the fig leaf got there first!

We do not have to look far to find reasons for all this guilt and unhappiness, because human beings carry a whole history of cruelty and anxiety around with them in this aspect of life. When we look at some of the terrifying things people do to satisfy the sexual drive, it's not surprising that some people, some generations, decided that the whole sexual instinct was at war with the soul. No doubt in each of us there are stored experiences which we would far rather had never happened.

But in the eyes of the Creator, who saw what He had made and "behold it was good", there can be no shame about the body nor any of the processes for which it was intended. He gave us our sexuality and He meant us to express it. I have suggested ways in which our understanding of our sexuality should change, and other ways in which we need to strengthen the traditional morality. All I want to say here, is that however we think again about sexuality in midlife, our decisions must be made in the soul as well as in the body. If there is cause for shame, it should be in the hurt we do to ourselves and to others, not in the existence of our sexuality. The sting of adultery is what it does to us, to our partners and our children. The sexuality must be the servant of our relationships, not vice versa. Our midlife decisions may well lead us to greater unhappiness if we get this wrong. We may deceive ourselves, blame everyone else, complain bitterly about how badly we've been treated, so as to justify our decisions, but in our soul we will often know that our choice was entirely selfish, and damaged us and others.

So it becomes even more important, in a world of fast-changing sexual mores, to keep our integrity. In this, prayer is very important. Prayer is not just something we do with our intellect, with our eyes shut, trying to block out bodily sensations. Prayer is an activity of body and soul. It involves the whole personality, from the soles of our feet to the top of our head. In a way, prayer is a sensuous experience. If we keep prayer firmly trapped in a form of words, or just in our brain, we cannot expect it to be integrated with the rest of us. It will not be surprising if our body lurches off in one direction and our soul in another. But this dichotomy won't work – we cannot serve two masters. We are looking for an integrity of personality. We hope to discover a unity of Body and Soul – where the physical self and the spiritual self are united. That is the test of what we should be doing.

Remembering always our capacity for self-deception, recall-
ing that we shall probably dis-integrate ourselves with monotonous regularity – in thought if not in deed – yet at the same
time, searching for love, self-control and then freedom.

6. *Searching for Our Centre*

It is a frightening experience for any human being to discover
that within himself he is a void. At every stage of life it is the
ultimate threat. I remember a fifteen-year-old girl lying on a
seat in a police station. She buried her face in the fold of that
seat where the back and the cushion met. She stayed like that
for an hour and we couldn't talk her out of it. Eventually she
sat up, and it was clear in talking with her that she considered
herself to be no person. I knew a boy called Chris who was
deaf, blind and dumb. He spent most of his day in a large
cardboard box, banging the sides. I think he was reminding
himself he was there.

I have met many people who said they felt unreal, that
somehow they were distant observers of themselves going
through the motions of living. They would do almost anything to slough off their skins to create some integrated feeling inside themselves.

These are extreme cases of what is an important search in
all our lives: the search for our own centre. There are people
who live completely through other people: their husband,
wife, children, parents. They have found it impossible to
create a sufficient identity to be resolutely and substantially a
person in their own right. The void can open up when they are
abandoned by the people who gave them their reason for
existence, or when the key person in their life dies. Gail
Sheehy's crisis was brought on by the realization that in one
sense she was totally alone:

How is it that accepting our essential aloneness allows us to
become more loving and devoted? It is because the dismay

of realizing that our safety does not reside in anyone else emboldens us to find security within ourselves.

Passages, p.416

Some children are so under the domination of their parents that they never find their own centre, and they become adults for whom so much seems at second hand. They begin to behave like leeches, needing to attach themselves and draw life from others. Some children are threatened by the void for the opposite reason. Their parents are empty and do not provide anything substantial for the children to test their selves upon.

Bereavement and tragedy can leave a great crater in our hearts, when for a time we are numb and void of feeling – that is a normal response. But for many people it is a way of life. It can take the form of the compulsive need to be with others, so that there is no capacity for solitude. It can result in a person always feeling that reality is what happens to other people. It can lie behind the superficial joviality of the life and soul of the party. We can be made to feel it when other people deny our value, or when no one hears our cries for help however loud we shout, when we are in the slavery of compulsive feeling. It can hit us when we suddenly see that our work is worthless, or taken away from us. It can be the direct result of a betrayal by someone we love. The void can open up inside us at almost every stage, and lead to such indiscretions as alcoholism, or drug addiction, or make us try to escape into more work, more food, more anxiety. Midlife produces some bad feelings of a void inside us, and may lead to emptiness in middle age and resentment in old age. Many factors tend to undermine our identity and provide us with false desti-nations. The steps which must be taken are those which enhance our identity, endue it with a strong sense of purpose, and support it with the love of friends. We have seen the many barriers to this essential strengthening in the centre of ourselves. In the end the most important change takes place within us. It is there where we need to discover the integrity of our personality, the assurance that we are truly the person we can be. I believe that this inward journey depends upon our relationship with God.

It is the great promised gift of religion. It is the promise that God will come and live in us. He will be our advocate – defend us against all that tries to destroy us. He will change our hearts where we need to grow in holiness. He will give us hope, and become so fused with us that His love becomes our centre. This is the ageless wonder of God which gives us the courage to be. It is indestructible.

7. *Through Fear of Falling*

I am indebted to an unpublished paper called "Through Fear of Falling". It studies the ageing process and refers to the great limitations in life which the fear of falling brings about. I have borrowed the expression to describe the earlier stage of the ageing process in midlife. A glance in the mirror, a string of funerals of parents and aunts and uncles, the withdrawal from sport, the threatened onset of the menopause, bring home to us our mortality. We have most of the Summer left, but the Autumn is following close behind. Many of us try in all sorts of ways to resist the natural process. We try to carry over the youthful "us" into middle age – "dressing up mutton as lamb", "he's over the top". We are just entering middle age and our next major upheaval may well be retirement, and then, after several more years, we shall die.

I have tried to show that failing to adjust during midlife can lead to even greater difficulties in old age. We should take care of our bodies – what we eat and drink and smoke. We must recognize that if we spend years resisting the ageing process at midlife, we shall probably fight it and be miserable about growing old in later years. We need to "see through" materialism and prosperity and power. They all have to be surrendered in the end, and for some of us quite a long time before the end. It is sensible to think – in so far as we can see ahead – where we will be, who we will be with, and what we will do when we retire. This is not to live constantly under a shadow, but rather to recognize that we may be retired for twenty or even thirty years, and we may have laid the wrong foundations. Can "he" cook, can "she" do the repairs? Is work the total sum of life? If so, why? Why not find and develop interests and creative skills which will not only fill out our own life, but give mutual shared interests and happy social contacts? It is perhaps time we put something back into the community – in politics, or community life or loving care. We should try to understand what mortality means to us – to face up to some ultimate questions about what we believe and what makes us tick. I have suggested that it is a time to renew the search for God if we have abandoned it, or to deepen our faith if we have it. What are the implications if there is nothing after we die, or if there is a new eternal life in God's dimension?

The great natural world surrounds us, and it provides the amazing garden for the second half of our life. It is one of the truly exciting facts of human life that until very old age – unless we become totally immobile – the night-scented stocks, the child sleeping in its cot, the racehorse cantering down to the start, the buzzard on "great pied mothwings borne along" – all these things retain their wonder. It was a joy to see my old dad smoking his pipe and looking out across the moor. It has been an honour to know the elderly people who go on discovering that the most beautiful exercise of prayer can go on filling us right to the end of our brain's control. These lifelong arts need practice, and they need priority – whether to relish the wonder of nature, or of man-made excellence, or to grow in that understanding and love of God which gives a hint of paradise. Ageing brings its pain and its limitations; midlife makes us sense the first real impact of the process. If we fight it and try to run up the down escalator, we shall probably have a heart attack, and in any case, it's going in the wrong direction. The fear of falling can be a cold wind across the soul, but if we embrace it, see it as the natural rhythm of our life and look towards our destiny, it will be a time of deepening our appreciation of life and the living of each day with a greater commitment and relish. It was Dostoevsky who said:

Love to throw thyself on the earth and kiss it. Kiss the earth and love it with an unceasing, consuming love.

Brothers Karamazov

Our life is a preparation for immortality where age is meaningless. So through faith in this life we can live with the light-heartedness of those who believe in eternity.

11

A Personal Postscript

I was surprised to discover whilst writing this book how many changes my own midlife brought about. Here is a list of the ones I can tell you about. I only hope that those near and dear to me might recognize at least some of them.

I decided that the "child" in me is valuable. I have to tackle the sulky bits and encourage the fun.

I recognized that I need not only God, but other human beings to know my worst and still love me. For this reason, I decided that everything serious about me should be known by somebody.

I recognized that satisfactions are transient, and often mutually exclusive.

I had to accept the insoluble, and hope that my small suffering helped somebody somewhere.

I tried to learn the lesson of the tree – seed, sapling, full strength, Autumn, Winter, for everything its season – saplings and gnarled trees both have their beauty.

Although authority remains a mystery, I learnt not to be dependent on those who exercise it; and in exercising it myself, I tried to realize that I was not always to blame – only sometimes.

I learnt that I cannot be on everyone's side.

I decided to allow myself a bit more anger.

I took up a new interest – painting – which is not dependent on muscle and wind.

I determined to look at the good bits in my paintings, and hope that one day they might fill the canvas.

I realized that I needed space of my own – both a place and a time.

I decided not to take my sins and failures so seriously – some of them are a bit comical.

I started to learn to cook and to renegotiate the domestic contract.

I gave up party political manifestos and tried to take the political implications of the Christian faith more seriously.

I determined to try and not be too depressed by certain politicians – Oh well, I can't achieve these changes overnight.

I determined to try to understand our racial attitudes and fight racism in practical ways.

I try to choose not to let my depression last through the night:

Tears may begin at nightfall
but joy comes in the morning.

Psalm 30:5

I realized that if I don't make time to pray – body and soul – I sink.

I know that work can be a demon as well as a blessing. When someone asks me what I'm doing on my day off, I respond happily that I'm having time off and it's great.

I keep on trying to understand why people don't always appreciate my being cheerful at breakfast.

If someone asked me to write a book, then I would do it – and hope that one day the good bits will stretch from cover to cover.

Bibliography

Bibliography

BERNE, E.	*Games People Play*	Penguin 1968
BONHOEFFER, D.	*Letters and Papers from Prison*	Fontana 1959 and SCM Press 1971
DYER, W.W.	*Your Erroneous Zones*	Sphere Books 1977
DE MELLO, A.	*The Song of the Bird*	Image Books 1984
EDINGER, E.F.	*The Creation of Consciousness*	Inner City Books 1984
GARBUTT, G.	*Through Fear of Falling*	Unpublished paper
GIDE, A.	*Journals 1889–1949*	Penguin 1967
HARRIS, A. & T.	*Staying O.K.*	Jonathan Cape 1985
HARRIS, T.	*I'm O.K. – You're O.K.*	Pan 1973
JUNG, C.G.	*Modern Man in Search of a Soul*	Routledge & Kegan Paul 1933
	The Undiscovered Self	Routledge & Kegan Paul 1958
KIERKEGAARD, S.	*Either/Or*	Anchor Books 1959
LAING, R.D.	*The Divided Self*	Pelican 1965
LEE, R.S.	*Freud and Christianity*	Pelican 1967
MOBERLEY, E.	*Homosexuality: A New Christian Ethic*	James Clarke & Co. 1983
MORRIS, D.	*The Naked Ape*	Corgi Books 1968
MUILENBERG, J.	*The Way of Israel*	Harper & Row 1961
NICHOLL, D.	*Holiness*	Darton, Longman & Todd
O'COLLINS, G.	*The Second Journey*	Paulist Press 1978
SHEEHY, G.	*Passages*	Bantam Books 1976
SOLZHENITSYN, A.	*One Word of Truth*	Bodley Head 1972
STORR, A.	*The Integrity of Personality*	Pelican 1963

SUTTEE, I.   *The Origins of Love*   Peregrine Books 1963
                    and Hate
WELSH, P.   *The Single Person*   Fairacres Publications
                                            1979

Unattributed Reports:
Homosexual Relations, Church Information Office 1979
Religious Hinduism: A Presentation and Appraisal, St Paul Publications 1964

Also available in Fount Paperbacks

The Mind of St Paul
WILLIAM BARCLAY

'There is a deceptive simplicity about this fine exposition of Pauline thought at once popular and deeply theological. The Hebrew and Greek backgrounds are described and all the main themes are lightly but fully treated.' *The Yorkshire Post*

The Plain Man Looks at the Beatitudes
WILLIAM BARCLAY

'. . . the author's easy style should render it . . . valuable and acceptable to the ordinary reader.' *Church Times*

The Plain Man Looks at the Lord's Prayer
WILLIAM BARCLAY

Professor Barclay shows how this prayer that Jesus gave to his disciples is at once a summary of Christian teaching and a pattern for all prayers.

The Plain Man's Guide to Ethics
WILLIAM BARCLAY

The author demonstrates beyond all possible doubt that the Ten Commandments are the most relevant document in the world today and are totally related to mankind's capacity to live and make sense of it all within a Christian context.

Ethics in a Permissive Society
WILLIAM BARCLAY

How do we as Christians deal with such problems as drug taking, the 'pill', alcohol, morality of all kinds, in a society whose members are often ignorant of the Church's teaching? Professor Barclay approaches a difficult and vexed question with his usual humanity and clarity, asking what Christ himself would say or do in our world today.

Also available in Fount Paperbacks

The Courage to Be
PAUL TILLICH

The problem of anxiety has dominated much of contemporary literature and philosophy. In this book Paul Tillich tries to point the way toward its conquest.

The True Wilderness
H. A. WILLIAMS

'In a time when the Christian Gospel so often appears unreal and irrelevant to the world, this shatteringly honest book must make a profound impact on all who read it . . .'

Gillian M. Burnett,
Methodist Recorder

Reaching Out
HENRI NOUWEN

A study full of rich spiritual and psychological insights offering stimulating reflections on the process of planning and living a life in and with the spirit.

Catholic Education Today

Chance and Necessity
JACQUES MONOD

'This is a great book, sinewy, lucid and intelligible alike to the non-scientist and the novice in philosophy.'

The Economist

Also available in Fount Paperbacks

Journey for a Soul
GEORGE APPLETON

'Wherever you turn in this inexpensive but extraordinarily valuable paperback you will benefit from sharing this man's pilgrimage of the soul.'

Methodist Recorder

The Imitation of Christ
THOMAS A KEMPIS

After the Bible, this is perhaps the most widely read book in the world. It describes the way of the follower of Christ – an intensely practical book, which faces the temptations and difficulties of daily life, but also describes the joys and helps which are found on the way.

Autobiography of a Saint: Thérèse of Lisieux
RONALD KNOX

'Ronald Knox has bequeathed us a wholly lucid, natural and enchanting version . . . the actual process of translating seems to have vanished, and a miracle wrought, as though St Teresa were speaking to us in English . . . his triumphant gift to posterity.'

G. B. Stern, The Sunday Times

The Way of a Disciple
GEORGE APPLETON

'. . . a lovely book and an immensely rewarding one . . . his prayers have proved of help to many.'

Donald Coggan

Fount Paperbacks

Fount is one of the leading paperback publishers of religious books and below are some of its recent titles.

- [ ] THE WAY OF ST FRANCIS Murray Bodo £2.50
- [ ] GATEWAY TO HOPE Maria Boulding £1.95
- [ ] LET PEACE DISTURB YOU Michael Buckley £1.95
- [ ] DEAR GOD, MOST OF THE TIME YOU'RE QUITE NICE Maggie Durran £1.95
- [ ] CHRISTIAN ENGLAND VOL 3 David L Edwards £4.95
- [ ] A DAZZLING DARKNESS Patrick Grant £3.95
- [ ] PRAYER AND THE PURSUIT OF HAPPINESS Richard Harries £1.95
- [ ] THE WAY OF THE CROSS Richard Holloway £1.95
- [ ] THE WOUNDED STAG William Johnston £2.50
- [ ] YES, LORD I BELIEVE Edmund Jones £1.75
- [ ] THE WORDS OF MARTIN LUTHER KING Coretta Scott King (Ed) £1.75
- [ ] BOXEN C S Lewis £4.95
- [ ] THE CASE AGAINST GOD Gerald Priestland £2.75
- [ ] A MARTYR FOR THE TRUTH Grazyna Sikorska £1.95
- [ ] PRAYERS IN LARGE PRINT Rita Snowden £2.50
- [ ] AN IMPOSSIBLE GOD Frank Topping £1.95
- [ ] WATER INTO WINE Stephen Verney £2.50

All Fount paperbacks are available at your bookshop or newsagent, or they can be ordered by post from Fount Paperbacks, Cash Sales Department, G.P.O. Box 29, Douglas, Isle of Man, British Isles. Please send purchase price, plus 15p per book, maximum postage £3. Customers outside the U.K. send purchase price, plus 15p per book. Cheque, postal or money order. No currency.

NAME (Block letters) _____

ADDRESS _____

_____